B

SPEAK OUT

LIZ: I *like* loving women. And I *like* loving men. The uniqueness comes with the individual, not the sex of the person.

RENÉE: Making love to a woman is like making love to myself . . . a total acceptance of my womanness. When I'm making love to a man, ideally the female principle and the male principle are trying to unify . . . a cosmic thing.

CINDY: To me being gay is as limiting as being straight. You can't be lovers with everybody, obviously, but we can experience a wide variety of things.

GRETCHEN: At times it's a difficult lifestyle because I feel alone, but at the same moment I realize it's extremely rewarding emotionally. I'm able to love more people more closely, and I don't mean just physically.

BENETIA: What I'm attracted to and excited by in men and women are their differences. I like women because they are soft and smooth. I like men because they're rough-skinned and hairy.

VIEW FROM ANOTHER CLOSET

Exploring Bisexuality in Women

Janet Bode

A KANGAROO BOOK
PUBLISHED BY POCKET BOOKS NEW YORK

VIEW FROM ANOTHER CLOSET

Hawthorn edition published 1976

POCKET BOOK edition published September, 1977

ISBN: 0-671-80972-5.
Library of Congress Catalog Card Number: 75-40583.
This POCKET BOOK edition is published by arrangement with Hawthorn Books, Inc. Copyright, ©, 1976, by Janet Bode. All rights reserved. This book, or portions thereof, may not be reproduced by any means without permission of the original publisher: Hawthorn Books, Inc., 260 Madison Avenue, New York, N.Y. 10016.

Printed in the U.S.A.

ACKNOWLEDGMENTS

Grateful acknowledgment is made to the following for permission to reprint material from copyright sources:

Bergler, Edmund. *Homosexuality: Disease or Way of Life.* New York: Hill & Wang, 1956.

"Bisexual Chic: Anyone Goes," excerpt from article. Copyright 1974 by Newsweek, Inc. All rights reserved. Reprinted by permission.

Deutsch, Helene. *The Pyschology of Women,* vol. 1. New York: Grune & Stratton, 1944, by permission.

Diner, Helen. *Mothers and Amazons: The First Feminine History of Culture.* Copyright © 1965 by Julian Press, Doubleday & Company.

Ford, Clellan S. and Beach, Frank A. *Patterns of Sexual Behavior.* New York: Harper & Row, 1951.

Gross, Amy. Excerpt from " 'We're the Thorn in Everyone's Side' . . . an inquiry into bisexuality." Copyright © 1973 by The Condé Nast Publications, Inc.

"The New Bisexuals," excerpts from article, reprinted by permission from *Time,* The Weekly Newsmagazine, copyright Time Inc.

Wolff, Charlotte. *Love Between Women.* New York: St. Martin's Press, Inc., 1971.

Acknowledgments

When I take on any major commitment the shrew-martyr facet of my character periodically surfaces. There is no adequate way to repay my family and friends for enduring me during those times. Words of deep thanks and appreciation are all I can offer to those—not necessarily in order of importance—who made the whole process easier for me.

Barbara Zaun first suggested my writing this book, helped me devise a chapter outline, and guided the initial direction of the manuscript. Her encouragement has been continuous, her insight invaluable.

Amy Hempel took my tear, soft drink and cigarette stained pages and returned them with ideas for changes. She curbed my penchant for redundancy and clarified my rambling sentences.

My father, Carl, supplied both professional advice and biased parental praise. My sisters, Barbara and Carolyn, added their enthusiasm, long distance, to keep me going. I always knew I could count on them, as well as on my stepmother, Charlotte, stepsister, Judy, and especially my stepbrother, Tony, who intuitively arrived on my doorstep whenever it was time to celebrate the completion of another chapter.

The support Carol Mayede gave me is impossible to summarize in a few sentences. She made sure I did not die of malnutrition (at last count I owed her 147 meals), she listened to my complaints, and she joined me when I stormed through the flat emitting small primal screams.

Catherine Sollecito provided her Capricorn wisdom and quiet reassurance, which stabilized my efforts. When I was in between homes Cindy Mitzel not only let me use her living room couch as a bed and her kitchen table as a makeshift desk, but also offered her typing services at bargain prices, and nonstop pep talks for free.

Barbara Althoff helped me to clear my head of life's clutter so I could get on with the work of writing. Johannes Ph. van den Brink has been a steady, reliable friend, always willing to listen to my problems as well as to share my triumphs. David Chesnick's daily calls to check on my sanity and progress gave me a work break and renewed my drive.

Josephine Hester contributed her knowledge of the classics and her suggestions on where to research this topic. My agent, Joan Naggar, deserves much praise for not making me feel guilty when I disappeared during a crucial month without telling her how to reach me.

Thanks go to those at the Ghirardelli Wine Cellar— my mental vacation resort and steady income during the months it took to write this book—and to the band and Crystal Pistol, conveyers of beautiful music for my leisure moments.

This book could never have become a reality without the women who allowed me to interview them. Many thanks to them for sharing their time and lives.

Finally, I wish to thank the person who created the space that needed to be filled with a time-consuming project such as this. Everything happens for a reason.

Contents

1.

From Myth
to Maturation

From somewhat structured consciousness-raising sessions to chats over the back fence, women are affirming that their own sexuality is not the taboo subject it once was. Many are approaching it with curiosity, honesty, experimentation, delight, and awe.

When the October 1974 issue of *Redbook* magazine featured a questionnaire concerning the sex lives of its readers, approximately one hundred thousand women completed the form. To put this number in context, the Kinsey report, which was done in the early 1950s, was based on interviews with about eight thousand women. Morris Hunt's book *Sexual Behavior in the 1970s* used data collected from 200 interviews and 2,026 questionnaires. The first conclusion reached by the *Redbook* staff was that "contemporary young women are comfortable with the subject of sex."

Mature women, as well as teen-agers and even some preadolescents, have moved from hesitant interest in themselves as sexual beings to acknowledgment of their feelings, outspoken opinions on the subject; and overt activity. Planned Parenthood workers have had to go through deep soul-searching about their policy of confidentiality when nine, ten, and eleven-year-olds come to their clinics requesting birth control information and devices. Women are wrestling with their sexuality as

11

adults and often, too, acting on their sexual feelings at an earlier age than did recent generations.

While heterosexual women are in the majority in our society, growing numbers of lesbians are announcing their sexual preference—not only coming out of the closet but slamming the door behind them to ensure that others notice their emergence.

Although we are moving at a snail's pace toward tolerance of alternate life-styles, we still tend to categorize people as either masculine or feminine, good or evil, active or passive—and, of course, heterosexual or homosexual. But in matters of sexual preference, as with other parts of a person's character, there is often a middle ground. For countless women the labels "straight" or "gay" simply are not applicable. These women relate to both men and women sexually and platonically. If labels must be used, bisexual is the most appropriate.

For many people the concept, possibility, and reality of bisexuality are nonexistent; but bisexuality does exist, and for that reason it should be examined and integrated into our culture. If the writings of a nation mirror its priorities and beliefs, then there has been minimal concern for or interest in bisexual women. Bisexuality did not appear as a topic category in the *Reader's Guide to Periodical Literature* until March 1973 and since that time only a few articles have been listed. And no libraries have a classification for bisexuality in their card files.

When you search through texts of mythology and the histories of differing societies, you realize that the allusions to this subject do not attach a specific word to it. Because women generally were not creating the literature of recording the history, we know more about the activities of men. One can only wonder what the women were experiencing. Even Elizabeth Gould Davis's excellent book *The First Sex* adds little information about the sexual life-styles of women through the ages. Davis offers ample proof that matriarchies flourished during ancient times, and that as men won

power and influence they rewrote the myths, changing
ruling goddesses first into hermaphrodites then into
gods. But she does not include sexual information
about mythological figures or mortal women.

The treatment of women in early Greek mythology
centered mainly on the changing relations between the
queen and her lovers. It then moved into portraying
women either in an unfavorable light or as victims of
kidnapping or attempted or actual rape. Aphrodite was
renowned for her promiscuity and adulterous conduct.
Eos seduced young mortals. Nymphs, one after another,
were abducted and seduced. The list of victims of
mythological male violence could begin with Leda and
lengthen through several distressing paragraphs.

Zeus is a classic example of bisexuality among gods.
Although married to Hera, he had numerous dalliances
on the side, including one with Ganymedes. Ganymedes,
the most beautiful youth alive, was selected by the gods
to be cupbearer for Zeus. When Zeus decided he also
wanted him as a lover, he disguised himself in eagle's
feathers and abducted him. This saga gained great
popularity in ancient Greece because it gave religious
justification for pederasty. (Eros at one time was hailed
as the god of pederasty; but there was no female equiv-
alent.) Another myth involving Zeus and Hera records
their disagreement as to which experienced more enjoyment from sexual intercourse. Tiresias, who had been
both male and female in his time, was called upon to
judge. He voted in favor of the woman.

Sappho is reality echoing mythology. She was generally viewed as exclusively homosexual but may actually
have been one of the first bisexuals of note in history.
Fragments of the poems she wrote in the seventh century B.C. still exist, and though she sometimes broods
over her betrayal by men and describes looking to
women for solace, she also mentions sexual appreciation of men. Yes, she loved women; but she had a
child, and in her bridal songs there is no negation of
heterosexual marriage.

We know the ancient Greeks paired young boys with

older warriors on the battlefield to deepen their sense of loyalty to each other. What has often been disregarded is that these mature men had wives and children in addition to their youthful male lovers. The tradition continued, and when the boys grew older they, too, married, became fathers, and then served as companions/lovers to the new recruits. It is not farfetched to conclude that some of the women who remained in the towns and cities also had love relationships with other women and equally could be defined as bisexual.

One custom that has been recorded about the activities of women revolves around the cult of Bacchus or Dionysus. As part of a religious experience, a means of achieving "enthusiasm" for and possession by the diety, respectable married matrons and their female offspring would journey into the surrounding hills for one or two days of drinking, dancing, and sexual explorations. Possibly because of its religious significance, this procedure was accepted by both men and women.

Human sexuality did not go hand in hand with feelings of guilt and shame during that era. L. J. Ludovici, in his book *The Final Inequality,* said pregnancies before marriage were explained away by being blamed on a handsome god in human form or river gods who manifested themselves while teen-agers were swimming. Homosexuality, generally mentioned only in reference to males, was considered a natural experience. By Plato's time love between men was not only accepted but often extolled, yet not to the extent of lessening attractions for women.

Helen Diner, in *Mothers and Amazons,* states that Spartan men and women often shared the same young lovers "free of jealousy. . . . Loving the same boy or girl, in turn, formed a common bond between their lovers, who competed in their ability to educate and promote their youthful friend." Marriage was illegal before the age of thirty and homosexuality prohibited after thirty-five. Sexual freedom was still the rule, and the wedding ceremony did not mean the beginning of an exclusive relationship.

By 146 B.C., when Rome annexed Greece, the Roman citizens had incorporated many of the Greek gods and attitudes into their culture. There might have been official disapproval of the Bacchic rites, but some practiced these, too. Ludovici also mentions that in Sulla's time (136–78 B.C.) the Isis cult appeared in Italy; it was believed to include lesbian experiences. Other ceremonies and rites briefly alluded to include married women relating to women on a sexual level. Thus, if the acts were religious in nature, bisexuality for women appears to have been integrated into the societal fabric.

The Romans of that period surrounded sexuality with an aura of common sense practicality. Sex was an appetite to be satisfied. Homosexuality never became as much of a cult as it was in Greece, but it was in evidence. Glimpses of upper-class women include their sojourns to fashionable resorts where they associated with transvestites, homosexual men, and female lovers. Livy (59 B.C.–A.D. 17) talks of clandestine groups with large memberships—mainly women and "effeminate" men who gathered for Bacchanalian festivals. Sex was for pleasure, not procreation.

And then the axe fell.

As the Jewish and Christian faiths permeated the land, so did the repression of women. The misogyny of St. Paul and many of his successors helped bring about the downfall of equality between the sexes. All women would suffer for what Eve had done to Adam. From the first century onward, self-denial, especially in regard to sexuality, was the rule. By the third century Anglo-Saxon law had itemized almost every type of sexual practice and matched it with a harsh punishment. Celibacy was considered the ideal, and virginity was exalted. Sexual intercourse was routinely banned on Sundays, Wednesdays, and Fridays, plus forty days before Easter and Christmas. There were sanctions against extramarital affairs, masturbation, thoughts of intercourse, and, needless to say, any homosexual experiences. It is obviously difficult to unearth any traces of bisexuality among women when sex in general was so disdained.

By the Middle Ages the status of women and the degree of equality varied among different societies. The Byzantine Empire was as repressive as some of the Western cultures, but there are accounts of women in harems who related to both sexes on all levels. However, in areas where women were burned alive for numerous reasons, including masturbation and loving their sisters, and returning crusaders were importing such inhuman practices as infibulation, clitoridectomies, and chastity belts, if any women were acting on their bisexuality they certainly were not doing so openly.

With the Norman Conquest the noose around sexuality loosened a bit, predominantly among the upper classes, but there were still twinges of guilt attached to it. We do not really know what was taking place among the young women who were sent to court to find spouses but who, while waiting, spent hours among the older women learning about life and—perhaps—love between women as well as men. The impact of the church began to soften as the philosophers of the European Renaissance replaced the laws of God with the laws of man. Women were elevated slightly in position and once more became desirable. The leisured people had time to explore each other's sensual and emotional feelings, and these were not solely restricted to members of the opposite sex. The first book of mainly erotic content published in Christian Europe, in about 1426, was called *Hermaphrodite* and dealt with a being that had both a penis and a vagina.

By the late 1600s and early 1700s gentility and passivity were again imposed on women. The straightjacket of oppression was wrapped around women as the cult of the hymen became so important once more that booklets were published on the art of identifying virgins. This attitude continued and increased until by the nineteenth century proper Victorians were capable of ignoring the network of brothels, obsession with flagellation, and defloration of virgins, and denying that women had any sexual interests or could enjoy the experience.

Margaret Mead in her *Redbook* magazine column wrote an article titled "Bisexuality: What's It All About?" in which she cited examples of bisexuality from the distant past as well as in more recent times, commenting that writers, artists, and musicians especially "cultivated bisexuality out of a delight with personality, regardless of race or class or sex." Mead mentioned those who went against the suffocating moral standards of the Victorian age and, later, the "international clusters of artists gathered on the Left Bank in Paris before and after World War I and the Bloomsbury set in London, all of them creative, innovative men and women, [who] were privately but quite frankly bisexual in their relationships." Mead believes that "perhaps the freest development of bisexuality has come about in the past in periods and among groups in which the cultivation of individuality has been a central value."

While there is historical evidence of bisexuality among Western cultures, few historians, sociologists, psychologists, and physicians have been willing to examine it. The scientific community has quietly recognized bisexuality for some time, but it has seldom been discussed as a possible alternative to heterosexuality or homosexuality. What limited theories the old-guard commentators have held are currently being questioned by such anthropologists as Mead, as well as by sex researchers and feminists. But both the defenders and the challengers have produced so little published material on the subject that research is often fruitless. A line here, a paragraph there, and no more. Books devoted to the study of human sexuality are nearly devoid of factual information about bisexuality.

One of the first medical men to theorize about bisexuality was Wilhelm Fliess, a devoted friend of Sigmund Freud, upon whom Fliess had tremendous influence from the mid-1890s to the early 1900s. Originally a nose and throat specialist, Fliess moved from his field and developed a bizarre method of numerology in order to "prove" the inherent bisexuality not only in all people but in each living cell. Because there are generally twenty-eight days between the beginning of each menstrual period and twenty-three between the end of one and the start of the next, these two numbers became pivotal to his theory of bisexuality. He determined that twenty-eight represented a female component and twenty-three a corresponding male part; therefore both were present in each cell. Thus we are all bisexual by nature. His views were not too widely acclaimed.

Wilhelm Stekel, another colleague of Freud's, gained greater acceptance and credibility for his theories, which were recorded in his book *Bisexual Love,* portions of which are still used in explanation or defense of bisexuality. Stekel proposed, "All persons originally are bisexual in their predisposition. There is no exception to this rule. Normal persons show a distinct bisexual period up to the age of puberty. The heterosexual then represses his homosexuality. He also sublimates a portion of his homosexual cravings in friendship, nationalism, social endeavors, gatherings, etc. If this sublimation fails him he becomes neurotic. Since no person overcomes completely his homosexual tendencies, everyone carries within himself the predisposition to a neurosis. The stronger the repression, the stronger also the neurotic reaction which may be powerful enough in its extreme form to lead to paranoia. If the heterosexuality is repressed, homosexuality comes to the forefront. In the case of the homosexual, the repressed and incompletely conquered heterosexuality furnishes the disposition to neurosis. The more thoroughly his heterosexuality is sublimated the more completely the homosexual presents the picture of a normal healthy person. He then resembles the normal heterosexual. But like the normal heterosexual individual even the 'male hero' type displays a permanent latent disposition to neurosis. The process of sublimation is more difficult in the case of the normal homosexual than in the case of the normal heterosexual. That is why this type is extremely rare and why a thorough analysis always discloses typical neurotic reactions. The neurotic reactions of repression are anxiety, shame, disgust and hatred (or scorn). The heterosexual is inspired with disgust at any homosexual acts. That proves his affectively determined negative attitude. The homosexual manifests the same feelings of disgust for women, showing him to be neurotic (or else he hates women). For the normal homosexual—if there be such a type—would be indifferent toward women. These generalizations already show that a healthy person must act as a bisexual being.

"There is no inborn homosexuality and no inborn heterosexuality. There is only *bisexuality*. Monosexuality already involves a predisposition to neurosis and in many cases stands for the neurosis proper."

More representative of the Freudian school is the view of the psychiatrist Helen Deutsch, who admitted there exists a bisexual phase during early puberty but stipulated that an extension of this must be considered an arrest in the individual's development. In volume 1 of her text *The Psychology of Women*, she explains bisexuality first in terms of triangles. These triangles can involve the love of two girls for one woman, three girls with each assuming differing roles, or the "more normal and more progressive . . . mixed triangle"— two females and one male. Deutsch also states, "The presence of a strongly bisexual tendency shortly before the conflicts of adolescence, that is, at its beginning, is less repressed in girls than in boys." Further, she believes that the greatest conflict arises not in the individual's concern over whether she loves men or women, but rather in questioning if she is a man or woman. She sees the "task of adolescence" as a time to overcome the Oedipus complex, the "primitive ties with the mother, and to end all bisexual wavering in favor of a definite heterosexual orientation." Her obvious conclusion is that bisexual women are abnormal.

Deutsch's work was originally published in 1944. More recent psychiatrists, psychologists, and psychotherapists have considered the subject of bisexuality in women in a somewhat broader context. Dr. Charlotte Wolff, who wrote *Love Between Women,* agrees with Deutsch that women may have a stronger tendency than men towards bisexuality, but she bases this assumption on the dual nature of female sexual organs. She also veers sharply away from the negative connotations that Deutsch applies to a continuation of this type of life-style. Wolff says, "In the very beginning of foetal life no differentiation of the sexes exists, and it is likely that memory traces of our early hermaphroditic structure never die. We certainly are bisexual creatures, and this innate disposition is reinforced by the indelible memory of childhood attachments, which know no limitation of sex." Rather than terming bisexual activities in adult life as being indicative of lack of development, she feels that they could be a positive step toward a better quality of life. "The one and only way to achieve equality and progress in human as well as love relationships lies in the expression of the whole bisexual nature of every man and woman."

As a survey of "expert" opinion continues, the only certainty is that there is no universal agreement on the origins, reasons, existence, normality, acceptability, and degree of bisexuality in women. Dr. Albert Ellis, executive director of the New York-based Institute for Rational Living, states that people who are exclusively homosexual or exclusively heterosexual are neurotic. Ellis's theories can be balanced against those of Dr. Edmund Bergler, a psychoanalyst whose work concentrated on the study of sexual problems. In his book *Homosexuality: Disease or Way of Life,* Bergler dismissed the possibility of bisexuality by asserting, "Bisexuality—a state that has no existence beyond the word itself—is an out-and-out fraud, involuntarily maintained by some naïve homosexuals and voluntarily perpetrated by some who are not so naïve." He concluded that belief in the existence of bisexuality is "as rational as declaring that a man can at the same time have cancer and perfect health."

The psychotherapist Dr. Leah Cahan Schaefer, a fellow of the executive board of the Society for the Scientific Study of Sex and author of *Women and Sex,* declares that the potential for bisexuality is present in everybody. We are all capable of reacting to differing kinds of sexual expression. Our environment guides us toward our choices of sexual orientation. Some of her views might be challenged by the society's president, Dr. John Money, head of the psychohormonal research unit at Johns Hopkins University. In a May 1974 *Time* magazine article he was quoted as saying, "Bisexuals generally do not have the capacity to fall in love with one person." They feel fondness, not love.

By late 1975 Money had altered his position somewhat. In a letter he elaborated on his theory of sexual orientation, stating that a person's psychosexual behavior is not a free-will choice, but rather one that is predetermined by a combination of prenatal hormones and influential experiences during the first eighteen months of life. Some people differentiate their "gender identity/ roles" so as to be exclusively heterosexual or homosexual, while others retain their original bipotentiality.

Money concludes with a humane suggestion for those caught in the forces of societal judgments against anything but the heterosexual norm by stating that nature is equally comfortable with all forms of sexual orientation, but society is not. His recommendation is to obey one's nature in order to develop fully one's "erotic potential, maintain erotic self-respect, and maximize the chances of a mutually exuberant erotic relationship."

Dr. Natalie Shainess, a Manhattan psychoanalyst, stresses that most bisexuals are either latent homosexuals or latent heterosexuals. In her view the rare bisexual is in dire straits, for "where you see true bisexuality, it is the result of great inner chaos and conflict. The sexual identity is fragile . . . she [the bisexual woman] is nothing, a yo-yo, looking for satisfaction and never finding it." Residues of Deutsch's ideas are seen in Shainess's writings as well; in Shainess's view, bisexuality (and homosexuality) are symptoms of "developmental damages" during childhood. While homosexuals grow up distrusting the opposite sex, bisexuals are in an even worse plight, because they do not trust either sex.

If a final tally had to be taken, those who deny the viability of a bisexual life-style would surely win. Though these views are bending a bit among anthropologists and sex researchers, most psychiatrists, psychoanalysts, and others do not accept bisexuality as a normal condition. This attitude perhaps reflects the latter group's concern with helping troubled individuals to become able to fit themselves into a specific society. The perspective inherent in dealing with individuals maladjusted to the demands of a single society must necessarily be more limited than that which evolves from dealing with a wide range of individuals in divergent societies. Hence the greater affirmation among anthropologists of the existence and acceptability of bisexuality.

The field of sex research also has been a little more open in its approach to bisexuality. Even though sex researchers deal with a specific society, they study what people actually do rather than what society says they should do. In addition, their data are broader than that of psychiatrists because they are chronicling the behavior of a large variety of people, from the "normal" to the "abnormal."

Besides Mead, two other anthropologists, Clellan S. Ford and Frank A. Beach, have mentioned the topic of bisexuality. Working at approximately the same time as Bergler, they conducted extensive research on sexual behavior, which they presented in their book *Patterns of Sexual Behavior*. Their findings include the fact that the difference between sexuality in humans and in animals is purely one of approval/nonapproval. They conclude, "A biological tendency for inversion of sexual behavior is inherent in most if not all mammals including the human species. . . . The basic mammalian capacity for sexual inversion tends to be obscured in societies like our own which forbid such behavior and classify it as unnatural." They also cite a questionnaire that was given to twelve hundred self-defined heterosexual women concerning their sex lives. Twenty-six percent of them had had some specifically homosexual experience.

Anthropologists offer evidence of cultures where bisexuality is a continuing custom and occurrence. Although these examples, such as the Batak people of northern Sumatra and many North African and Turkish societies, are not generally familiar to the average American, they show that our Western condemnation is not universal. But few authorities have taken this lifestyle seriously enough to even write about it. This holds true also for the majority of sex researchers; Kinsey et al. were exceptions.

In 1953 the authors of *Sexual Behavior in the Human Female* pointed out that there are some persons whose "psychosexual reactions and socio-sexual activities are directed, throughout their lives" towards individuals of the same sex, just as there are those whose reactions and activities are directed toward individuals of the opposite sex. "These are the extreme patterns which are labeled homosexuality and heterosexuality. There remain, however, among both females and males, a considerable number of persons who include both homosexual and heterosexual responses and/or activities in their histories. Sometimes their homosexual and heterosexual contacts occur at different periods in their lives; sometimes they occur coincidentally. This group of persons is identified in the literature as bisexual." Kinsey went on to emphasize that the fact that there are individuals of this nature is one of "which many people are unaware; and many of those who are academically aware of it still fail to comprehend the realities of the situation."

In accordance with the observation that exclusive heterosexuality and exclusive homosexuality are extremes of a continuum, Kinsey's study graded the participants on a scale of zero to six, zero representing exclusive heterosexuality and six representing exclusive homosexuality. He found that by the age of forty, 19 percent of the women in the total sample had had some form of homosexual experience. These women tended to be older and better educated than the majority, and most were single.

After that, silence on this subject from the sex researchers. Masters and Johnson have yet to examine this form of human sexuality. Hunt's *Sexual Behavior in the 1970s* includes twelve pages of references for bestiality, probably a less widespread occurrence than bisexuality; and yet bisexuality is not even indexed. Therefore the body of professional writing has been both slim and contradictory.

With the increasing impetus of the women's movement, feminists have begun exploring this topic, but with many of the same prejudices as the experts. Too often they have been hesitant to accept the concept of other sexual life-styles. At one women's meeting the attendants were asked to declare with which of the two camps—heterosexual or homosexual—they aligned themselves. There was no mention of the existence of other options, such as bisexuality or celibacy.

But that was two years ago. Now many people are beginning to acknowledge that there are women who are bisexual and to consider (1) what we can learn from them, and (2) whether they need any type of support.

Some see our society's rigid enforcement of heterosexuality as a product and means of continuation of sexual oppression. Betty Roszak, a feminist writer, advocates an androgynous society, because "from the bedroom to the boardroom to the international conference table, separateness, differentiation, opposition, exclusion, antithesis have been the cause and goal of the male politics of power. Human characteristics belonging to the entire species have been crystallized out of the living flow of human experience and made into either/or categories." She concludes that it is the male habit to set up these boundary lines, based on clearly defined differences. In her opinion the sex response is a primitive one and "there is no differentiation between man or woman . . . just a shared organism responding to touch, smell, taste, sound. The sexual response can be seen as one part of the species' total response to and participation in, the environment."

Lately the media have begun to recognize the existence of bisexuality as a life-style, though not always with any degree of gravity. *Newsweek* featured an article in its May 1974 issue entitled "Bisexual Chic: Anyone Goes." The piece treated what has been a way of life for some people for many years as a sensational fad. There was a statement from Joan Baez about a female love of hers, an explanation that bisexuality was "inevitable" because as "his-and-her clothes, hair styles and role assignments blurred the line between the sexes until they overlapped, the only thing left to swap was sex itself." The regulation number of experts were trotted out with their quotations decrying this "new" happening. *Time* magazine discovered the topic that same month, adding its longer list of famous bisexuals and surprisingly focusing on women (Janis Joplin, Tallulah Bankhead, Dorothy Thompson, and Maria Schneider). The article then countered that option with a stable of psychiatrists, psychologists, and other observers who collectively shook their heads in dismay over what these poor women were doing to themselves.

In the fall of 1975 Barbara Walters devoted a week to bisexuality on her television program "Not for Women Only." For once there was a more balanced presentation, with bisexual people talking about themselves. They were a diverse group, who could not have had their sexual preference pinpointed at forty paces. They showed the viewing audience that bisexual women, like their exclusively straight or gay friends, come in all shapes, sizes, and marital states.

And it is this factor that is unsettling to many people. Bisexual women do not slip readily into any assigned category. They refute the signposts that declare that if a woman is married, especially with a child or two tossed in, obviously she is heterosexual. They counter the theory that all single females with short hair who wear hiking boots and overalls are lesbians.

Times are changing, even if the acknowledgment, understanding, and acceptance of bisexuality are coming slowly. Now you can pick up newspapers and journals from major cities across the country and find announcements of bisexual rap groups, workshops, and poetry readings. A meeting for bisexual women in Berkeley, California, had sixty participants—half were married. There is a larger, ongoing organization in New York City called Bisexual Liberation Center, whose membership includes both sexes.

But despite this greater openness, bisexuality remains shrouded in mystery even to bisexuals themselves. Those who have searched for a more thorough insight through reading are stymied by the lack of sources. What they discover is not a definitive body of information but jarring controversy. For some this inability to clearly define themselves causes unwarranted confusion and fear of their own sexuality. For others it results in amused acceptance, because they are "label-phobians," glad that society cannot attach a classification to them. These women express a feeling of being in limbo. Although they do not necessarily want a peg on which to hang their identities, they are curious to know if their experiences are unique or if there are others in our culture functioning as they do.

Bisexual feminists are often criticized by both gay and straight segments of the movement. This double rejection produces one of several reactions: the acknowledged bisexual woman may fulfill only one set of desires, relating sexually only to men or only to women; she may become a closet bisexual—living secretly as a bisexual but appearing to the world as a heterosexual; or she may, in a twist illustrated by Kate Millett in *Flying,* live as a closet bisexual in the gay world.

Until recently no one cared to investigate this field. Now there is interest, but the data are minimal, much of them based on hunches, guesses, and gut feelings. What emerges is a host of contradictory and confusing statements: Bisexual women are incapable of loving anyone, so they desperately turn to both sexes in hopes of fulfillment; they are the most adjusted individuals, because they own up to their dual sexuality; they are freaks; they can never make a clear-cut decision about anything, let alone their sexual preference; they are exceptional because they can love and enjoy people as individuals rather than basing their emotions on gender differences; they are pleasure-seekers, groping toward excitement in the fad of anyone's bed for fun and frolic; the bisexual population is large and growing; there are not any more bisexuals today than there were twenty years ago, it is just easier to declare your sexual orientation; bisexuality is a disaster for culture and society; the best world would be one in which everyone were permitted to act upon his or her true bisexual nature; people are either gay or straight, pretending to be bisexual is just an easy shield to hide behind to alleviate pressure and emotional trauma; the "sex" in the word "bisexual" has been greatly overemphasized— bisexuality is just one more element of an individual's being.

Which statements are closest to the truth? The answer, like the life-styles of the women themselves, lies somewhere in between. For information we should turn first to these women, the primary source and true authorities on this subject.

I consulted the women who provided the information for this book in two ways—through a six-page questionnaire and in personal interviews generally lasting several hours. Usually the interviews took place in the women's home or in mine. We talked across a kitchen table or while sitting on a couch. In the beginning a few mentioned that they were somewhat ill at ease. I was a stranger who would be not only listening to incredibly personal information, but recording, editing, and synthesizing it. To relieve this strain I spent time explaining the basic purpose and scope of the book, as well as the types of questions I would be asking. I emphasized that the women could refuse to answer any of the questions. As the interviews progressed, they relaxed. Tension, silence, pathos, humor—our emotions swung pendulumlike as the minutes went by.

Many of the respondents guided the conversations by bringing up ideas they felt were vital and valid in defining their identities. Most stated they wanted to share their life histories but remain anonymous. Therefore, though the stories are true, the names are fictitious. People ask how I found the women to interview. Initially I went to friends who had suggested this topic. Among them was Stella, who said she was willing to talk if I would help her rearrange her furniture. (She is the kind of person who is first to offer her seat to others on a crowded bus.) The interview lasted longer than we had intended, so she gave me a rain check on my moving services. Then there was Melanie, who sat cross-legged on a cane-back chair during the entire taping session. Her main movements centered on relocating her matches, lighting her cigarettes, and trying to keep the remnants from overflowing her portable ashtray. She blamed her heavy smoking on attending too many boring meetings.

There was Benetia, continually volunteering to do those jobs no one else wanted to do. And Doris, the coupon-clipper—before we could start she had to check the morning newspaper for the latest discounts. Another friend, Liz, has those 1930s good looks—flat-planed face, red, heart-shaped mouth, perfect, minute nose, and conscientiously plucked crescent eyebrows. They recommended other women, who directed me to still others. They opened their homes and their lives to me. Merlin and I hovered near the electric heater in her cavernous living room. The twelve-foot high ceilings swallowed what warmth was generated by the late afternoon sun. From her front bay window we had a view of a park. We heard shouts from a neighborhood football game as we talked. Sometimes, when she discovers a stray bulge of fat on her normally slender frame, she goes out and joins those games.

I interviewed Patricia in her combination minicommune, work, and living space. She and three other women were converting a small warehouse into a habitable location. To walk from the front door to the daybed/couch you had to leapfrog your way over a maze of photography equipment, a pool table, and boxes of cooking utensils, clothes, and books. The women had recently moved in and were still building shelves and combing thrift stores for dressers. Unlike most interviews, which were done on a one-to-one basis, Patricia preferred to have her friends present. Afterwards we moved into a short evaluation where all of us discussed the questions we felt were most important and the ones they'd thought I would ask that I hadn't.

Fran's interview was conducted in the back booth of a coffee shop near her suburban home. It was during the early evening hours, so business was slow and we were left undisturbed. Although the waitress must have wondered what was going on, she discreetly maintained her distance as we took two hours to nibble our way through our pie a la mode. Fran projects a somewhat matronly image—she feels it is necessary for her line of work. On weekends and vacations, she mentioned, her truer self appears as she relaxes in jeans and sweaters.

I had met Annette once before at a Halloween party when she was an aspirin, complete with white wig and a spray-painted plywood circle encasing her torso. I had not seen her since, and we laughed about the different personalities she takes on depending on her mood. Whatever she does she attacks with all her energy and enthusiasm. When she is at work as a buyer for a large department store, she will put in overtime without pay because she strives for perfection. When she plays, she's equally determined to have a good time.

Gretchen's interview lasted three hours and could have gone on longer if I had not run out of tapes. She said she loved having a captive audience and thoroughly enjoyed talking about herself. During the conversation she gave her Old English sheepdog, Robin, his weekly brushing. She used to do it almost daily until she got bored with the process. Her original diligence came from reading an article that said sheepdogs shed enough in one year to make a full-length coat. That fact prompted her to save all of Robin's hair for nearly a month before she realized she did not want to card, spin, and knit a coat for herself or anyone else.

Other women responded to the notices I placed in newspapers or the flyers I sent to women's centers. Michele, an intense and sometimes strident feminist socialist, called after talking to an acquaintance who had been interviewed. The bulletin board in Michele's farm kitchen was layered with lists of the division of work among the people living in the house and announcements of rallies and meetings. When I met her she was collecting unemployment but assisting at a day-care center four mornings a week. Cindy, who has the type of high cheekbones, regally thin nose, and reed-thin body that photographers praise so highly, heard about the project through a friend.

Jackie saw a flyer and called me. She provided qualifiers to many of her answers and then added that because she is a Libra she is compelled to look at all sides of any issue. At first she responded hesitantly, but after about a half hour she visibly unwound and explained her concern that I would only ask about the sexual side of bisexuality. Renée was attending a workshop at a women's center when she heard about this book. When we got together she was starving her way through her second diet of the year. She wavers between wanting to be gaunt and gaining weight to hide herself behind mounds of flesh. She said her weight was an important factor in her life and an indicator of how she felt about herself and her sexuality.

The women I talked to are kind and good. The majority are interesting, bright, articulate, and witty. Some people that I discussed this book with challenged the credibility of women who recounted their lives. My only response was, what would they gain by lying?

When the talk ended we all agreed that even though professionals had treated the subject of bisexuality gingerly, it was time for a candid look at this nature of women. I am prejudiced on two counts. I think bisexuality is a viable life-style. And I am a feminist and want to aid in the process of women's understanding of each other. This book is not a scientific study with control groups and extensive charts. It is the recorded experiences and philosophies of bisexual women. By speaking for themselves, they provide a view from another closet.

2.

Sum of the Parts

Convene a meeting of the women interviewed for this book and they would wonder, along with the casual observer, what their common denominator was. Without labels identifying their bond of bisexuality, few surface characteristics link them together. There would not be a wild aura of sexual tension seething through the room. The physically glamorous and flamboyant would not outnumber the less attractive women present. You would see neither an abundance of high-fashion styles nor of weathered jeans. They are women you would meet in your neighborhood, run into on the street, call on the phone, work with you on your job, turn to for help, make your friends.

Although the average age of the participants was 27.8, there were several teen-agers and quite a few over forty. There was variance in the educational level, but the majority had more formal schooling than the national average. Nearly 85 percent had completed some college, and of that total 33 percent had bachelor's degrees, 30 percent master's and nearly 10 percent had either worked toward their doctorates, were now enrolled in graduate programs, or had obtained a Ph.D. Four percent were high school dropouts; others were high school graduates. Some were still students, though most had left that road behind them.

Those employed represented an incredible diversity of occupations. Some worked in creative fields such as music, art, theater, and writing; others were clerks, secretaries, teachers, and laboratory assistants. Among the participants were a university counselor, an occupational therapist, a sex therapist, and a free-lance filmmaker. There was a biostatistician who was currently supporting herself by prostitution; the president of a small corporation who often had difficulty meeting her payroll; an office manager who felt secure as her weekly paycheck came in; a welfare recipient barely surviving each month; and a graphic artist who owned her own business and home. About 10 percent were unemployed but actively searching for work.

Where and how the women lived reflected their economic status. Most were supporting themselves. Their homes ranged from tightly confined studio apartments in the city to opulent, sprawling houses in the suburbs. Furnishings included everything from early Salvation Army to Scandinavian modern. Some of the women were stereotypes of the American dream of comfortable happiness with two cars in the driveway, color televisions, twice-yearly vacations. Others rejected any outward status symbols, concerning themselves with spiritual fulfillment.

Only 17 percent of those interviewed were currently married, but 23 percent had been married at one time. Those marriages had ended by divorce, annulment, or the spouse's death. The women who had been divorced stated that their bisexuality was not a factor. Ten percent had been married more than once, and one woman had had three husbands. The majority, approximately 60 percent, had never married, and many said that although they had lived with an individual over extended periods of time they had no intention of following societal dictates on this point either. Some had children. Others wanted them, but at a later date. Quite a few planned never to have children.

For those interested in astrology, there were more Geminis and Cancers, with Virgos following close behind. The air and water signs outnumbered earth or fire.

That there are differences among bisexual women is apparent, but are there similarities? To begin at the beginning, there is the question of whether sexual orientation is determined by prenatal hormones or environment. The experts do not agree on an answer to the classic clash of nature versus nurture. Dr. John Money emphasizes nature's influence, saying that by adulthood our sexual life-styles are static. Dr. Wardell Pomeroy, who was at the Kinsey Institute for well over a decade and is now in private practice in New York City, is often the spokesperson for the opposing view. Pomeroy says he has found no evidence for hormonal predisposing of sexual orientation. Our sexual interests and outlets can always, and at any time within reason, change.

Let's leave the professionals behind and consult the bisexual women. None of them was a psychiatrist, psychologist, or even sociologist, but their input has merit. They did not want to be treated as if they were guinea pigs or laboratory organisms ready for dissection, microscopic exploration, and theoretical analysis. When we exchanged ideas we talked as friends, women helping women learn more about each other.

Barely 10 percent agreed with Money's opinion. The language they used to describe their feelings was not couched in scientific jargon; there were no semantic frills. Kay, thirty-four, the younger of two children, spoke from practical experience and her own insight. "I believe our sexuality is strictly genetic. If through genes someone can be gay, a little less male genes on one side and more female or vice versa can make someone bisexual. The best example I've seen of this is two friends who've gone through sex-change operations. When you meet men who are obviously women except they have male genitals, you realize nature did something—their genes were crossed. Those people are women, unfortunately with testicles and penis. When genes can carry you that far, genes also make you bi-, homo-, or heterosexual. How can anyone get upset by other's sexuality? It's not choice. I understand why they're the way they are, therefore they should comprehend why I'm where I am."

Jackie's short response represented the more widespread opinion, "I don't give any credibility to the hormonal theory."

What the overwhelming majority believed is that we are all bisexual by nature. It is society's conditioning that channels most people into a heterosexual life-style. Without that force we would find greater variety and acceptance. The women discussed not only cultural pressure but their family backgrounds, too. Are there patterns in those early childhood environments that shaped the way they live today?

Sweeping generalizations are dangerous, restrictive, and misleading. Bisexual women are individuals. Because they have rebelled against one of our culture's strongest rules by actively relating to both sexes, they also wince at the concept that a precise profile will emerge from their differing histories. In addition, those willing to share their stories may be far from average; thus any concrete percentages must be considered with caution instead of firmly grasped as gospel. Each statement of "fact" can be placed side by side with a qualifying phrase. Each "expert's" opinion can be backed up by examples or just as easily disclaimed by countering samples.

FAMILY BACKGROUND

Into what kinds of families were the women born? Eighty percent were *not* products of broken homes. They had the regulation mother and father who remained married to each other at least until their children became adults, though there were sharp differences in the quality of their parents' relationships. When asked to evaluate that, some settled for single-word descriptions—"mediocre," "tense," "uncommunicative," "stormy," "pressured." Almost 65 percent stated that in retrospect they would question the love between their parents. Some added that they understood why their parents did not divorce, but in many cases they believed divorce would have been better for everyone involved. Many of those who felt this way were feminists and were convinced their mothers should not have let themselves be trapped into their traditional roles. They could have stood up for their rights, demanded help around the house, and sought more active assistance in raising the children.

One woman, Patricia, from a Latin background, was adamant in her views on unfairness in her family. "According to my father's machismo theory, he was the head of the household and could do anything he wanted. My mother was supposed to lower her eyes in obedience while devoting her life to the home, church, and kids. His manhood gave him the leeway to justify his extramarital affairs and lack of responsibility in the day-to-day upbringing of the children."

Merlin, a graphic artist, did not think her parents would have been better off if they had gone their separate ways, but she did summarize the quality of their relationship as "terrible." "To me it was always dull, because they were hostile to each other without actually fighting. There wasn't yelling or screaming, but the undercurrent of tension was always present."

Many of the women who felt their parents set a poor example of a firm relationship explained their judgments in terms of their expectations of themselves. As adults they set high standards for dealing with other people on an emotional/intellectual level, and it is often difficult for parents to measure up to their current standards. If they did not value personal relationships so highly, perhaps they would not evaluate their parents as harshly.

Some women discussed their parents' relationships at length, while others offered only brief statements. Susan said, "My parents were never close. After thirty years they still live in the same house, but they've created a situation where they don't see each other often. I don't know why they married in the first place, let alone stayed together as long as they have."

Mutual respect was something that concerned Karen, twenty-six and single. "Marrying my father was something my mother did to rebel against her parents. On different levels neither of them had any respect for one another. My father, because he was a man; my mother, because she was better educated. I never felt completely at ease with either of them."

A few of the women had never taken time to consider the interaction between their parents. They were simply entities who were there to provide them with a roof over their heads, clothes on their backs, and food in their stomachs. As Renée recalled, "They were just my mother and father. There might have been a relationship, but it had evaporated by the time I was conscious of such things."

With an intake of breath, Ann, twenty-four, an office manager, leaned back and asked, "How extended an answer do you want? I've thought about it quite a bit." Then she smiled. "There wasn't a total absence of affection, but I'd never say my home was a calming environment. A ritual developed that continues even now. First the argument, then my father disappeared for a few days. My mother wouldn't panic, because he always came back after he'd had a chance to sort things out. Sure enough, by the third day he'd waltz back in, and everything would stabilize until the next blow-up about six months later."

Childhoods recalled with pleasure balanced those remembered with pain. About 15 percent classified those early years as "boringly content." There was warmth and affection in the household. They felt secure in the love of their parents for each other as well as for them. Time passed with no major traumas. Melanie's mouth widened into a magnetic grin. "My childhood was enveloped in love. Everyone touched and hugged a lot in my family. I had support when I needed it, discipline when I deserved it. Since my consciousness has been raised by the women's movement, I've felt touches of resentment toward the life my mother had to lead. Now I think she compromised too much, although when we talk about it, she says it was worth it. She does agree her full potential as a woman might have been limited in her marriage, but she loves my father. He appreciates her. Together they've created a good life."

Maria was equally enthusiastic about the example set by her parents and the atmosphere they created. "They reminded me," she said, "of an image from the book *Cat's Cradle,* two people totally completing each other. My relationship to them had to be different, because I was obviously going to be independent of them when I became older. In my romantic eyes I pictured us as temporarily united voyagers through life."

About 20 percent of those interviewed were raised by single parents. In some instances the women had been sent to live with foster families, grandparents, aunts, or uncles. Liz referred to her parents' divorce as a "seismic kind of thing." She continued, "My father immediately remarried, and then there was a tug-of-war throughout high school between the two of them. My brother and I were subtly called upon to select sides. I felt closer to my father, but only because I perceived him as the victim somehow. He needed— I don't know what—maybe reassurance."

Bouncing back and forth between relatives and strangers is difficult for any child. Benetia's mother and father were divorced when she was six. Until the age of ten she lived with her mother; then she went to live with her father for a year. Next it was back to her mother, on to a foster home during the school year, return to her mother. But what she wanted emphasized is that she survived and is now an extremely happy woman with a home, husband, two children, and a career. Her conflict and anger arose from having to assume greater responsibility in the various homes where she lived rather than from being shuttled from one location to another. "My mother had to work three jobs to support us, and that meant I had to do the washing, ironing, cooking, shopping, everything. It put me in a position of authority over my brothers, and I used that authority because I felt it. When I was living with semi-strangers, I didn't know what role to assume. Was I a child, an adult, unpaid help? There are many parts of my childhood I simply don't remember. In many ways I feel as if I lost my youth in the shuffle of growing up."

Where parents divorced when the children were young, the women admitted that their memories were colored by the comments their mothers made about their fathers. In Sally's case, her father abandoned his family when she was four and her younger brother was one. Sally's only recollections were that she "was afraid of him and felt guilty about that. Mother told me my father relied very heavily on her and she wasn't that strong. I really don't know much about it. After he left I only saw him once a year, so my opinions are marginal. Obviously the quality of their relationship was poor, or they would have stayed together.

"Being raised by a single parent doesn't mean you grow up without love. Because my mother didn't have to divide her energy between husband and children, she seemed to have more affection to offer us."

Money—or the lack of it—plays a part in the dynamics of any family. Estimating their parents' economic status, nearly 60 percent of the women judged themselves either in the lower or lower-middle-class bracket. General terms were used, without dollar amounts attached to them because the majority did not know how much their parents earned. They based their responses on the types of neighborhoods in which they lived, manner in which they were dressed, variety of food available, and kinds of luxury items in the homes. Again there were sharp differences. One woman's childhood environment included a governess and housekeeper; another, the daughter of a nonunion laborer, had been ill fed and shabbily dressed. One's father had been a mechanic, another a lawyer. In some cases both parents were employed. There were blue-collar workers and professionals. There were garbagemen, businessmen, corporation executives, salespeople, secretaries, nurses, policemen, and plumbers. Some women endured periods during which neither parent was employed. Many understood that there had not been much money around the house, but they had not felt deprived. Others recalled with bitterness the poverty of their youth. This was true of Helen.

Helen was raised on a farm in a rural area of the Midwest. Now in her late forties, she lives comfortably with her second husband and three children. But the emotions she connects with her early years surfaced as she talked. "That poverty is something I'll never forget. During the depression my father worked for a dollar a day as a trucker when he could get it. He'd been an electrician but lost that job and never held another one until the war came. Then he made good money, but he spent it all on himself. He turned himself into a brute and my mother into a subjugated, neurotic, desperate, trapped doormat.

"After he left the farm for a while to work salvage on one of those war jobs, my brothers and I ran the whole show to help out my mother. We never seemed to have enough food to eat or decent clothes to wear. Now I care for both my parents, but I'm still bitter for the hell they made out of my childhood."

Doris also felt her family's low economic position caused her problems. In reaction against that early tension, she has ensured her own financial security as an adult. She surrounds herself with what she calls her "toys"—a stereo, color television, expensive skis. "I will not allow myself to fall into the same bind that held my parents for so many years. I can still remember lying in bed at night and hearing arguments about money. By a young age I knew the whole billing cycle of dunning letters. Sometimes they'd make me answer the phone or door when they thought it might be some collection agent. I work hard for my money, have no credit cards, and only buy things when I can afford them. How can anyone hope to establish meaningful relations when one's tummy's roaring and the only choice is gruel or warmed-over rice with gravy? That single issue of bills caused such anger and fury in my household. It taught me that you can't count on men to be providers, either. Women must be just as capable of supporting themselves."

Granted family income level does not influence future sexual preference—what is worth noting is that the majority did not come from affluent backgrounds. They were evenly divided on whether this enhanced or detracted from their home lives. About half of those interviewed felt that if you do not have much money in a family you have to look to each other for entertainment and enjoyment. You cannot play tennis, go sailing, or take a Sunday drive in the country. Therefore you have to be more creative and work harder at experiencing those around you. This carries over to your adult years as you search for contentment through and with people rather than material possessions. Doris represented the other half. She pointed out that when your family's priority is daily survival, there are fewer moments of relaxation and happiness from spending time together.

PARENTAL DOMINANCE

As the exchange of ideas continued, I questioned each woman about which parent was dominant. Approximately 20 percent flatly refused to answer. They did not want to be part of the "smother-mother" or "weak-father" game. In explaining her reticence Jackie said, "I get so irritated with studies of anybody not marching to society's main drummer when the 'experts' blame their actions on one of their parents. And the finger always seems to be pointed squarely at dear old mom. Sure my mother had a lot of influence on me, but that was because she was around more than my father."

Of those who answered, 65 percent stated that their

mothers had been more dominant in their children's lives, but they didn't necessarily dominate their spouses. Many qualified this in a similar manner to Jackie's. Their mothers were dominant by default. The kids spent more time with their mothers than with their fathers. Generally neither parent scored high points in terms of offering substantial love, warmth, and attention. Less than half spoke of love for their mothers or being openly loved in return. Many missed a feeling of support. In examples of secure environments trouble began to simmer during adolescence, with disagreements about school, clothes, and dating. Yet more than half said their current relationships with their mothers were cordial and good. Sometimes this is a long-distance love because they have moved away from their families. But it is love nonetheless.

When reviewing their interactions with their fathers, the women fell into the pattern of early affection turning to lessening or withdrawal of emotional security and physical attention around the ages of ten to thirteen. Again, others said they never felt love or any degree of involvement with their fathers at any time. About 20 percent of the respondents believed their fathers played a stronger part in their lives. The remainder judged both parents exerted a like amount of control. One woman reported that *she* was the central figure in her life.

Gretchen was one who expressed ambiguity about her parents' influence on her. "I don't know which one was dominant, but the impression my father gave me, the idea I grew up with, was my mother was very domineering. I know there's a difference in the words, but the resulting actions are the same. She wanted control and authority. Being the man, he felt she was undercutting his masculinity.

"For many years I didn't like my mother, and it seemed to be mutual. Then, beginning at sixteen, there was growing admiration on both sides. I respect her for the struggles she had and overcame. I'm able to see her as a friend, another human being. My father was the dominant emotional image. He was my idol; someone I loved, looked up to, and emulated. Those weren't emotions I aimed toward mother. She was the rule-maker and enforcer. She had the greater influence on what I did with my day-to-day life. As I said, I like her now, whereas I'm still hung up about my father. He's not an idol any longer. He's not a perfect person. I haven't grown up in my relationship to him."

About 20 percent of the group came from homes where one parent—generally the father—was an alcoholic. Colleen felt the alcohol factor contributed to her feelings about her parents. She was an only child, raised in the suburbs. "My parents each had their own way of coping with problems and with me, which was not necessarily together. Dad might have been dominant in the work world, but once he walked in the door he'd withdraw into a protective shell of liquor. For years when I'd wonder why he wasn't eating with us, I was told it was because he was asleep. Only much later did I figure out his sleeping translated into the fact he was drunk or passed out. My mother did most of the raising of me, the disciplining, the praising. I suppose mom and dad talked, but I didn't see a whole lot of it. I suppose they fought, but I didn't see that either.

"Even though I was an introspective child who tried to please my parents, I felt so removed from them. Mom was supportive and caring in a guardian sense, but she wasn't a very affectionate or demonstrative person. My craving for physical warmth and just plain contact was something neither of them seemed capable of fulfilling. When all I wanted was a hug, mom would back off saying, 'I've had enough.' I began to find the contact I needed by holding walls. They became my substitute substance, my outlet for touch. There was another side to mom in that she was helpful emotionally. I played the piano and could always count on her to praise me for a piece I'd played. Dad would usually walk out."

Very few felt the physical loneliness and isolation that Colleen talked about. They were not now seeking love from anybody to make up for that void in their formative years. More discussed love-hate feelings toward their parents. Barbara, a striking, dark-haired woman of twenty-seven, typified this attitude: "My mother could create intense love-hate conflicts in me. Her temper was terrible, and sometimes she'd use straps on me or hit my head against the wall. I truly didn't believe I'd acted badly enough to provoke that wrath in her. Yet on other occasions I remember her bathing me, or she'd comb my hair and reveal a great depth of caring for me.

"I know this sounds as if my mother was an evil person, but that's not true. My father was into running around, and she had to find some outlet for her anger. For a long time I had no respect for my father. He'd zip through money and women faster than any man I've seen since. Okay, I'm an adult and things are in better perspective. Now I understand where they were coming from and why they treated each other and me the way they did. It's a much better atmosphere. Things have settled down; but moving away from home certainly helped me love them more."

In the 35 percent of the cases where the women originally evaluated the quality of their parents' relationship as "good" or "fine," a carryover took place. They generally judged their feelings toward their parents in positive terms, too. Cindy said her parents have "one of the best marriages" she has seen. "They gave each other a lot of space, but in the right way."

She continued, "I don't know if I'm typical or not, but I love my parents. My mother was more influential on my behavior, and I felt closer to her. If you weighed interest, she'd win out over my father. There was the normal dose of tension as I got into junior high, but then my mother went back to school, and that helped. Instead of being repressive, she wanted to know what I was doing for my own safety. Yelling was one of her favorite pastimes. It was funny, because she screamed about both good and bad things. Pretty soon I learned not to let it bother me. When my father yelled, it was a big deal—'Hey, he's paying attention to me. I must have done something really bad.' This was during junior high, and I'm sure all kids are beasts then. Those were the years the only time I could get his attention was when I'd done something wrong. There was more distance between my father and me. He let me do what I wanted to, where my mother sometimes wanted to channel me too much for my liking.

"My mother was always curious about everything I was doing, while my father's curiosity seemed to dry up in comparison to hers. Once we had a huge scene because of this. I wanted him to care about me more often than when I'd made a mistake. By nature he was a quieter, more reserved kind of person. At the same time I thought he felt things more deeply than my mother. Sometimes my mother seemed superficial, flighty. What it comes down to now, they had different ways of expressing themselves. They both feel things. They're a complement to each other. My mother deals in practicalities; my father, in the artistic. He's into adventures, going out in the world and exploring. Because they balanced each other, they made me into a more balanced person."

You cannot isolate a single characteristic in people's backgrounds and declare that is what molded them into what they are today. The sum total of the parts is the issue. Nancy mentioned this and wanted a list of the variety of influences attached to her name. She was one of two children, but her brother died a lingering death from leukemia. Prior to his illness, the family had been very close. But with the increasing strain of the disease, her father withdrew from Nancy, and her mother began drinking. Nancy had loved her brother deeply and suffered from his death.

"All of those combined to sock me with mixed emotions toward my mother and father. I was at a stage when I needed mother, but she had to lean on the bottle and on me. She'd been a very home-oriented woman who didn't know anything except her family. My brother's debilitating disease took her already weak ego and demolished it. Up until I was about seven or eight I was my father's little darling; he lavished affection on me. Then, when my brother became sick, he pulled back his emotional support. During that whole four-year period he didn't pay much attention to me at all.

"After my brother died my parents sent me to live with my paternal grandparents, and during that period I tried to understand that my mother and father just wanted each other. When I was fifteen, they decided we should all live together again, but it wasn't a smooth adjustment. You can't automatically turn on a faucet marked love.

"Sometimes I feel my father tried to treat me as a logical, reasoning adult at too early an age. I'd always been independent and somewhat secretive, so many people thought I could take care of myself; but really I couldn't. It was a facade, and emotionally I was still a kid. He didn't take into consideration how raw my feelings were because of the upheavals in my early life. On the other hand, my mother wasn't always much help either. I began to lose respect for her because that period from eight to twelve was an important time of my life. When I should have had her help in refining my intelligence, I'd have to be walking her home because she was too drunk to make it on her own. Love? Hate? I don't know which."

A woman who did not see dominance of one parent over another definitely felt more influence from her father. "I liked him a lot more than I liked my mother. He's a chuckly, impish kind of man who didn't pay a lot of attention to me—but when he did, it was very intense. When he talked to me I knew he was directing all his energy to me, and that was it. Of course my mother, like any woman, had to be more fractured because she was trying to run a house, hold a job, and raise me and my brother. I knew she cared, but I never got any warmth from her. My father gave me that and also let me know I was one of the most special people in his life. I had a big impact on him.

"Yes, we had arguments, the regular parental-control growing up kind, but throughout it all I think we both knew we were each others' favorite person, and nothing could change that."

SIBLING RELATIONSHIPS

Most of the women interviewed for this book were born after 1944. Considering that this was during the postwar baby boom, the average number of children in the families is somewhat low—2.6—though the range is from one to as many as nine. Nearly 70 percent of the women were either the oldest or only child. Several others had circumstances such as the death of an older sibling or a large age difference (six or more years) between themselves and the next child, which made their upbringing similar to that of an oldest or only child. Some women suggested that first-born or only children tend to be more experimental in all areas, not solely their sexuality, so this predominance should not be surprising.

Of those in the category of oldest or only child, several believe their fathers wished they had been boys. Fran, an only child, brought this up during her interview. She said, "I used to think my dad wanted a boy, because I was more encouraged to engage in physical activities than in sedentary ones. There wasn't any resentment on my part about it, though. It got to the point where I'd be the one fussing about wearing dresses. My father'd say, 'Go put on some slacks.'

"When I was five my great-aunt came to live with us. She'd been raised in a European atmosphere and been taught that proper young ladies wore frilly clothes and curtsied to greet their elders. To get her off my back, I acquiesced and became that type of child when she was around. I learned early to do that. I believe that's why it's comfortable for me to be in two worlds now, both gay and straight, since I'm accustomed to the appearances game.

"Lately I've come to realize it wasn't so much that I was an only child or not a boy, but that my father was incapable of dealing with any children he might have had."

Patricia touched on this as well. "To understand my upbringing," she began, "you have to remember the dichotomy between the male and female in the Latin culture. My father was very conscious of being a man. With the birth of each baby girl in our family there was more and more unspoken yet very real desire on his part for a son. There should be someone to carry on the name, follow in his father's footsteps. While I didn't try to be a substitute for the nonexistent male child, I was aware of the fact he would have preferred me to be a boy."

There was irony in Michele's voice as she recalled her parents' disappointment that she was a girl. "When I was very little my mother told me they'd already had the name David picked out for their first baby. It wasn't either David or Michele, just David. It was as if they hadn't even thought about my being a girl. I'm sure my father would have liked someone real rough-and-ready to play with. By the time I was about twelve he joined one of those big brother programs for boys who don't have fathers. I felt left out, but he was the type of salesman who was charming with everyone but his family. There didn't seem to be much I could do."

Only 5 percent of the women who discussed this part of their childhood expressed any feelings of role-confusion or subconscious pressure to be either a boy or both a son and daughter. One of those rare exceptions was Maria.

At first she only completed a questionnaire, but based on her responses there was a follow-up interview. She is extremely articulate, with a bubbling sense of humor. Words did not come hesitantly but flew at lightning speed. Maria was born in 1947, the older of two children. She was raised in many different locations, but primarily in North Carolina and Tennessee.

She is hard to forget. Her lithe frame reveals the

daily exercise regimen she began a year ago. The image she gives is of a powerful person very much in control of herself. She began by describing the role her brother played in her life.

"A factor which had a tremendous influence on both my parents and myself was my brother. He was born severely retarded and at the age of four was placed in a home for 'exceptionals.' Even though I tried to do a thorough job of blocking him from my memory, he was the albatross around my neck. When I was eighteen someone asked when he was institutionalized, and I had no idea. Often I didn't feel capable of determining whether I loved or hated him.

"For me, it was what he was instead of who he was that caused turmoil. One of the reasons my family was tight was that we three shared a secret guilt for this 'mistake' that had been born. We all felt responsible for him, and perhaps I did the most. This is nothing I ever communicated to my mother or father, but there's a lot of evidence in my mind to back it up. Much of what I did when I was growing up was done trying to replace him. I became two children. The reason I consciously spent time with my father was because I felt the need to fulfill the part of son.

"We became pals who'd wander off to exotic places —the kinds a man would usually take his son. He didn't want me to be the typical Southern, empty-headed female. A couple of years ago he told me, 'Maria, I brought you up so you could fix the toilet if it broke. That's the kind of daughter I wanted to have.' I can fix toilets, and I feel good about it.

"My mother and I had this fantasy when we were traveling of growing older and more united to each other. We'd see people who'd begun to physically resemble each other because they'd become so close and we'd say, 'There we are in fifty years.' I saw myself as a fulcrum, delicately balancing my vulnerable parents.

"As far as I was concerned, my brother's existence wasn't totally bad, but it certainly created a situation that changed my life and the type of person I became. I lived for my parents as the two of us. I was a very good child who never misbehaved. I sensed the pressure my parents lived under because of their absent son and didn't want to rock their emotional boat.

"When my brother died at the age of twenty-two, I hadn't seen him for years. Maybe I had a feeling of loss, of sadness, but mainly there was tremendous relief for no longer having to be two people. I could just be me, not try to be the ideal or the son that wasn't."

For each example of sibling rivalry there were examples of fondness and friendship. Many described stages during which they liked their brothers or sisters and times when they fought continuously. Some women had to assume the role of mother for younger brothers and sisters. Others regretted that they had been only children.

SELF-IMAGE

Although many females go through a period of vaguely wishing they were boys, approximately 20 percent of those queried had sharp, specific memories. This question was not originally asked, but when several women began interjecting their feelings on the subject I began to include it. Joyce was one of the first to talk about it. "When I played games as a kid I'd take the roles that were more likely to be filled by men. Being an astronaut, a disc jockey, or a good football player appealed to me. I had to force myself to play house. Most of the time I wouldn't be the wife. Didn't want to be the mommy because it didn't seem like fun to me.

"I can still remember later on feeling I was very ugly and thinking maybe I would have made a good-looking guy. I'd look in a mirror, pull my hair back and say to myself, 'What a doll, this would have been good looks for a guy.' I think I was about fourteen at the time, and all the talk and competition for boys' attention was heavy at that age."

Many of the women who felt the most strongly about being a boy said this was in reaction to their parents' desire for a son. Children are very intuitive, they pointed out, and can sense much that parents do not communicate. One woman was born when her parents were in their mid-thirties. First they were overjoyed just to have a child, but then she believes there was a shift in their attitudes. "Initially my father spent a lot of time with me, breaking me into boy-type things. He raised me as a son up until a certain point, so I tried to fit into that. Then he abandoned me quite abruptly as it became obvious that I was a little girl. I wasn't sure in what direction to turn to regain his favor. Sometimes I'd try to be a son, and other times I'd be more interested in playing typical games with my girl friends."

In second grade Jackie idolized a cowboy hero. "I used to fantasize what it would be like to be that kind of person. I went so far as to sign some of my school papers with his name. There were other times when I wanted to be a boy, but it had very little to do with sexuality. Boys seemed freer to me, and I envied their activity."

The much greater number, about 80 percent, either had never wished they had been born males or had only done so for a short period of time. But then and now they are glad they are women. Elaine summarized her feelings from the viewpoint of her childhood years. "Looking back, I distinctly remember saying 'I'm glad I'm not a boy!' It first struck me when I was about eight and was cashing in on the advantages of being female. My brother had to work when he was a teenager, but I didn't. Even then I knew he felt the pressure of eventually having to be a breadwinner, and I technically didn't have to worry about that. I was very aware there were all kinds of expectations for my brother that there weren't for me. I watched how he had to deal with his male friends, how he had to be macho. I knew I didn't have to do that. I went through a period where I thought the worst thing in the world would be to be a man—that would be horrible because you'd have to be all these things that nobody wants to be. Nobody wants to be tougher than their friends. No one wants to be pushed into a box where they can never cry or hug a friend of the same sex."

As children, most played with trucks as well as dolls. Some became expert tree climbers, while others made sure they never got their clothes dirty. About 15 percent considered themselves very introverted and withdrawn. They spent most of their spare time reading or in solitary diversions. Others remembered they had preferred "boys'" activities to the more passive "girls'," but they had not been openly criticized for that. Where there was pressure to conform to stereotypical roles, it more often came from outside the family than from within. The majority, approximately 75 percent, were expressly raised to fulfill the role of female in American society. Until the last ten years there was not as much outspoken questioning of those preconceived images, so whatever rebellion the women employed was on a subtler plane, without a name attached to it. Maybe they did not want to play house, dolls, and tea parties, but they were not sure why. They were divided fifty-fifty as to those classified as tomboys and those who viewed themselves as typical little girls.

Brenda, the second of two children, commented on this. While numerous questions were needed to open up some of the women, Brenda immediately took charge of the interview. She seemed capable of carrying on several diverse operations at once. As she rambled through the anecdotes of her life, she removed one coat of nail polish, applied a fresh coat of bright orange, and waved her hands back and forth to dry the varnish. Periodically she would get up to remove a withered leaf from one of her thirty-seven (she kept count) houseplants.

An observer might have called her flashy. With admirable ease, she balanced on her three-inch platform sandals. It was hard not to notice her knee socks covered with incredible jungle scenes. She had decorated her blue jeans with wild needlepoint designs of sunburst, dragons, and birds. On her otherwise plain green turtleneck sweater, she wore a rhinestone pin.

"Now I dress to create an effect and flaunt my sexuality, but I was always somewhat belligerent even when I was a little kid. If someone wanted me to be your typical sweet thing, the wheels would start cranking and out would pop the opposite reaction. Sexual differences had no meaning for me at that age. I'd play hide-and-seek with all the neighbors, and to confuse whoever was 'it' I'd switch shirts with one of the boys so the players would think I was someone else. I never got embarrassed about changing clothes behind the bushes with some kid, never thought of it sexually until it was pointed out to me—that is, when the adults found out about it. Whammy, another thing I wasn't supposed to do.

"I wore pants to school every day until fourth grade, but it was because they were more comfortable. Why should there be any hassle? My parents were accepting in that they didn't really give a damn. Then one day someone from school called, and my parents did suffer from other people's delusions about me. This nameless school voice prodded, 'We're worried about Brenda because she wears pants every day.' They suddenly had a dress code that stated no girls could wear slacks after fourth grade. That was one of the few times I fell for society's pushing me around; instead of sticking up for my rights and wearing what I wanted to, I gave in.

"I think I was more into boys' games because I had an older brother. It was a double-edged thing, though. There was only eighteen months difference in our ages, but physically I grew up faster than he did. We were the same height for a number of years and ran around like buddies. Not only did I want to keep up with him, I wanted to surpass him. He was more introverted, almost a child prodigy. He taught himself to read at three. He had no time for sports, so I could outdo him there. At one time I even assumed the role of protective older child. When the kids in the neighborhood called him four-eyes and sissy, I'd beat them up for him. I never did think of it as my being the tough male and his being the weaker sex. I just did it."

RELIGIOUS INFLUENCE

Additional factors and side issues arose in the interviews as the women expanded their answers to the basic questions or suggested new ones. Many, especially those raised as Catholics, held strong opinions about the impact of religion on their lives, including their sexuality. Gretchen explained that she did not want to belabor the point but Catholicism meant that religion played a large part in her sexual development, or "actually lack of it," as she put it.

"It seems that Catholics are so interested in sex because abstinence until marriage is continually pounded into our heads. We have to think it's something fantastic, since it's such a forbidden fruit. What happens is we religious fanatics become overly sexual when we finally break through this repression. That's what made me run into group sex and all kinds of crazy things for awhile. After being told so often how damaging premarital sex was, I wanted to know; I demanded of myself that I discover what it was all about."

Ann felt it important to discuss her Catholicism as well. "At the parochial school I attended there was continual pressure to be a good little girl. That's not startling, but the way in which they did it was so distorted in my mind. When it came to sex, we were taught the whole shame and guilt aspect. Even now, at twenty-eight, I may have shreds of it in my subconscious. Right along with my personal development of having childlike sexual feelings, was the church-imposed development of guilt. The theory of mortification of the flesh was stressed. The martyr approach that to feel good was bad was always imposed on me.

Eventually I split from the school and the church. I became violently anti-Catholic. Only recently have my feelings mellowed and smoothed out."

Even though Jeannie was not Catholic, she attended a Catholic boarding school for three years. She felt the same ways as Ann about the lasting effect religion had on her. For Jeannie the influence went beyond the church alone to include the entire atmosphere created by the nuns, being surrounded by females, and living away from home. Many of the students came from broken homes similar to hers, and she found comfort in that. "There were no health or sex education classes in my school. We weren't allowed to see boys, so I missed out on all that adolescent boy-girl thing. After I left some of my friends would ask me what it was like there, and I knew from their voices they were sure there was rampant homosexuality going on. They were disappointed when I told them no.

"The closest I could come to that personally was when I felt love for one of my teachers. I always wanted to be close to her, have her touch me in some way, but I didn't relate to it sexually. What affects me still is the guilt on certain moral issues. Sometimes I consider going back there, saying, 'This is what I'm doing. What do you think?' I'd like to see what their reaction would be now, because they might have changed since those terrible days."

Religion influenced Michele's early life, but in a way not mentioned by any of the other women. "From the time I was seven until the time I was fourteen, I always wanted to kill myself. Every day I debated over whether or not to do it. The thing that kept me from it was that if you commit murder, you're going to go to hell. My mother wasn't a fundamentalist, so I didn't think it was literally fire and brimstone. I thought God would have this giant hypodermic needle to shoot me up with something that would make me feel even worse than I already did. And it would be hell. Maybe my religion saved my life."

SEXUAL IDENTITY

As the interviews moved from topic to topic I heard hysterical giggles and derisive sarcasm in response to whether the women thought their parents were heterosexual. Down the line they answered yes. Only about 5 percent mentioned a close relative who was homosexual. Helen included these thoughts about her parents' sexual orientation. "It would never have occurred to my mother that there was anything to be but heterosexual. My father was warped by his vision of sexuality. He was terrified one of his sons would not be man enough. I remember once he bullied my younger brother because he wore a green shirt and that was what homosexuals wore. The other brother he practically beat one time when he asked for a doll for Christmas. He was only four. What difference would it have made?

"What's strange is he was very tolerant of me. When I asked for toy cowboy guns my mother had a fit, but he said I could have anything my brothers had as long as I played with it. Once my brother said I couldn't fly airplanes, since girls didn't do that. My father went and pulled out a picture of Amelia Earhart, and the matter was settled."

There were occasional comments about their parents' appearances, such as "my mother looked kind of masculine," or "I sometimes wondered about my father." Elaine elaborated, "My parents were definitely straight, morally as well as sexually. Once my father heard that my brother and sister-in-law were dancing nude in their living room. He said he didn't think she was 'that kind of a girl.' Another time I mentioned something to my mother about orgasms and she said, 'What's that?' She didn't have any idea what marriage entailed. Nobody ever told her. After they got married my father wanted to have sex with her, but she locked herself in the bathroom. It wasn't until six months later that she consented; she talked to a priest and he told her it was her duty and that procreation was the purpose of marriage. That's the only reason she submitted, and that's how she looked at sex."

One respondent suggested that there might have been more openness about nudity and sexuality in her household than in homes from which exclusively heterosexual or homosexual children came. She wondered if this would hold true for the others interviewed. But those who talked about this aspect of their lives generally felt there was no more or less openness than in other homes. One stated she was sure her mother had learned the "facts of life on the delivery table." Another commented that since there were two children in the family her parents must have had intercourse twice. She could not imagine it happening more often. One's father was a biologist, and reproduction and gender differences were talked about frequently but mainly as related to his professional interests.

ENVIRONMENTAL INFLUENCES

After the women had talked about their childhoods, I asked if they felt there was anything in their early environment that had contributed to their sexual orientation. The answers varied as much as the women.

Elaine explained, "I never thought backgrounds had much to do with being bisexual. I think it has more to do with being an adult. I'm open to new ideas. That's how I became bisexual. It never seemed to have any roots in my childhood. I was never aware of any real longings as a child or at any stage for a woman to have sex with until after I had had sex with women. It wasn't until after that experience that I realized I liked it. As a kid I preferred to be with boys more than girls. Certainly after I had my daughter I enjoyed being with men more than women, because I couldn't tolerate all the talking the women did about children. Between tea, television, and kids, the topics were so narrow I was bored. I never would have suspected myself as a bisexual from where I was coming from. I'd been only heterosexual."

Merlin capsulized it as, "Only my own curiosity. My family was not intellectual. Actually my father was anti-intellectual, and my mother certainly never was a great reader or thinker. But I always wanted to know about everything. I tried to figure out why people did things and if I couldn't, I did them myself to get first-hand knowledge."

Melanie gave the primary credit to her mother, who was responsible for her being "terribly independent and self-reliant from a very early age. She and my father were strict on some issues but lenient on others. They didn't allow me out late at night, but they gave me freedom to do other things. They let me get married before I was twenty-one even though they didn't like the guy. My mother and her family probably broadened my vision. One of her brothers and her only sister are openly gay and have been for years. My aunt, whom I love very much, has been with the same lover for twenty years. To me, differing sexual preferences seem so natural. We didn't discuss it, because it was just there."

Another woman, Michele, proposed two theories. Her first opinion is unique and is included for that reason. "My mother told me that when I was born, I cried just once to get air in my lungs and then I was quiet. In other words I didn't come out screaming my head off. Yet I have the birthmark on my forehead, so I was pulled out with forceps. Maybe it's possible that my birth wasn't as bad as most people's and that has made me more capable of being open to new experiences. A more solid theory for me is that because I was never in one place long enough to really get to be friends with anyone, I was definitely a loner. I never developed a feel like most people have for certain customs being so basic. I was uninformed, I didn't pick up on a lot of social expectations that people have, so I didn't feel confined by having to live up to any."

Jeannie believed her family environment had the opposite effect to that planned. "I was so closed off from other people until I went away to high school. The years I was most open to suggestion were spent in a restricted existence up in the woods in Oregon. Those around me said I should have an early marriage, produce kids, and settle down to be a housewife. After high school I returned home and found it was the same as when I'd gone away. They were still right where I had left them. They didn't want me to go out. I was too young to get a job. One day I walked away, literally, and said I was going to lead my own life my way."

Several women recalled they had thought about the effect of their environments on their sexual orientation but had not come to any conclusions. Another said, "Let the exclusively straight ones tell why they've never carried through on their feelings for love for someone of the same sex. Then I'll investigate my background from that standpoint."

Stella thought that because of her environment she learned to be "curious about so many things. I believe unless I try something, how can I say anything about it. So I try things. Every now and then I get myself in farther than I thought I would!"

Judith had no firm conclusions. "I think I'm a fairly social person and that superficially I'm the kind who's gregarious. That comes from moving around—New York, Missouri, Kentucky, Maine, Pennsylvania. My parents also encouraged us three kids to be very adaptable. As far as my sexuality goes, I can honestly say it was never from copying my parents. I never felt any sexuality from either of them. Seldom was there any physical affection between them. Whatever developed in me seems to have been on my own. Where I got my attitudes about sex, I don't know."

Some women mentioned negative influences from their childhoods. They had been raised strictly, with many rules and regulations. After being held captive by their parents' example of a bad relationship, the women decided that learning to deal with people on all levels was important. Alicia felt her early environment in a "strong German, rural, Midwest community" was detrimental. "My parents are typical of that kind of attitude, that sex isn't good. I, and most of my peers in high school, didn't start dating until senior year at the earliest. My mother was nervous about sexual issues. She couldn't possibly have dealt with her daughters' questions.

"The whole area was populated by first and second generation German-Americans. We all came from farm families and were Lutherans. All my parents' socializing occurred at church. That place was so tight, so closed. If anything, for my first twenty years it retarded my sexual growth. I don't know whether there's an answer in all that, but that's what happened."

Renée, an only child from a Jewish family, had some ideas. "My parents always told me everything I wanted to know about sex. When I began dating there was talk about whether I should go out with Jewish bums versus Gentile bums. But the main thing they pushed was I should know what was good for me. They encouraged me in everything I did. My parents were coming from two different mental places, but both their opinions sank in. My father always told me to take care of number one, myself. My mother said to help other people. I came out somewhere in between in my attitudes. I've always gotten along with all kinds of people, no matter what sex they are. As I grew up I enlarged on my feelings for individuals and determined not to hamper myself in any way by gender."

Before answering, Annette paused. Then she leaned forward in her large, overstuffed chair and said, "I'm just doing what comes naturally. We've all been both male and female in past lives, and we reach a point when we can relate sexually to both because we've been both. This happens to different people at different times. Another thing that has helped me is I was taught, and have a strong belief in, love as a positive force. I learned as a child by the example set by my parents that it's important to love deeply and well."

Nature or nurture? The sum of the parts? No one knows or agrees—not the experts nor the bisexual women. Because it is impossible to investigate prenatal hormones now, we can only explore environmental influences to look for similarities. Take a checklist of contributing factors, consider each time more than 50 percent answered in the same general way, and this is what we find.

The majority of these bisexual women are well educated, single, and come from nuclear, unbroken homes with parents who were behaviorally heterosexual. They felt that the quality of their parents' relationship was poor. Their family's economic bracket was estimated as lower or lower-middle class. Their mothers were the dominant figures in their lives. They were oldest or only children, raised in the stereotypical manner regarding their roles as females.

But we should not lock these generalities around all bisexual women any more than reverse the process and believe that all who fall within these fuzzy margins are bisexual.

3.

Was It Good
for You, Too?

Everyone's development includes the discovery of sexuality. The day arrives when we realize the bodies of the two sexes are not quite the same. And we are curious. Almost 80 percent of the bisexual women interviewed felt there was nothing unusual about their early sexual explorations. They played doctor right along with the rest of the children in the neighborhood. They were no more passive or aggressive in comparing notes about what those differences might mean. They learned about sex from whichever source was most helpful and open—sometimes their parents, other times friends. They wondered where babies came from and were told "from the cabbage patch," or "the stork," or were given detailed factual explanations. Some consulted books around the house, but often these did not clear up all their questions.

As they grew older there were slumber parties, mixed parties, friendships with boys and girls. Sometimes the young girls practiced kissing so they would "know what to do with the boys." Spin-the-bottle, post office—these are universal pastimes. Most were concerned about the size of their busts, which were always too large or too small. Others wondered what menstruation was all about. As young teen-agers, many experimented with sex while remaining technical virgins.

The other 20 percent did not feel they had been more sexually active than the average—but they did believe their experiences were unusual. When Merlin was thirteen she began to collect soft-core pornography. She did not hesitate when she talked about her hobby, she merely included it as part of her childhood memories. "The only things available then would be somebody's older brother's *Playboy, Stud,* or some other tacky magazine. I'd bring them home until finally I had a whole envelope full. Sometimes I'd cut pictures out from Frederick's of Hollywood. I kept them in my bottom drawer and used to get them out when I masturbated.

"I seemed to know I shouldn't masturbate, but I enjoyed it. I didn't think I was perverted, so I decided masturbation must be human, normal, and healthy. One day I went to look for my envelope and it was gone. I wasn't about to ask around the house if anyone had seen it! But that didn't stop me from masturbating."

Renée, now an aspiring actress, thought she might have been more sexually precocious than most because, she recalled, "I discovered my sexual organ at five. I think I had my first orgasm then, too. Of course I didn't know it was an orgasm, but I remember being very surprised. At five I used to have fantasies when I was in bed. They'd stop short of actual intercourse. We would be sort of rubbing each other, and that's as far as I'd let myself go. I suppose I must have had an idea of what intercourse might be because I remember thinking we'd be close together. There'd be no penetration in my fantasy. It's really amazing when I think about it. When I had that first orgasm I was thinking about a psychiatrist, but I'd never even seen one. After it happened I told my mother that I'd been in bed and there was this weird feeling. She didn't dismiss it, but she didn't get upset.

"When I was eight or nine I'd get together with two of my girl friends. We'd kiss and touch. We'd pretend one of us was a boy. It was sexual as far as I was concerned, but at the same time I always knew there were boys out there as well as girls. I was exploring my sexual feelings and it just happened more girls were around, so that's where I went."

Elaine, who is thirty-five and divorced, with two children, mentioned an episode from her childhood. She felt adults would consider it sexual, but as a child she did not. "I lived in an isolated area where there weren't a lot of kids around. A girl moved in who was exactly my age. I admired her. It was puppy love. Nobody noticed because we were only twelve and girl friends could be close. She and I would do a mutual masturbation, although it was at night and in the dark. Nothing was ever said about it. It just happened, surrealistically. We'd sleep nude together, touch, and masturbate each other to climax. Somehow for me that was never a sexual experience. I never thought of it as 'sex' or 'orgasm.' As kids there're lots of things that happen to you that surprise you. You don't know how they got there. I didn't know where it came from, and I didn't really want to duplicate it. I didn't think about it at all."

Anyone who has had sexual intercourse can tell about the first time. In reference to this I left room for interpretation. The question asked about the first sexual "experience." The women could define this however they wanted.

Approximately 15 percent received their introduction to sex, other than that initiated by their own natural curiosity, in a blatantly disturbing and frightening manner. Between the ages of five to eleven, Amy had been molested by her father on several occasions. At the age of thirteen, to avenge her father's actions, she began actively seeking out sexual partners. The others in this category were victims of attempted or actual rape when they were adolescents. Their reactions to these occurrences were highly individual. One woman believed she later turned to men to mentally erase any negative connotations she retained because of the rape, while others internalized what had happened. Some, such as Benetia, felt that because they had been so young they attached minimal sexual feelings to the experiences. Now they think of them as acts of aggression rather than anything sexual.

Helen, who was raped thirty-five years ago, clipped her reply: "I had my first sexual experience at the age of thirteen, but it was rape. That I'd prefer not to talk about. If you leave out the rape, I was seventeen and with a woman. But it wouldn't have been with a woman if it hadn't been for the rape."

A few, such as Brenda, did not know how to answer. "Sometimes I don't know what to describe as my first sexual experience, because I had a couple of things happen to me when I was young that were primarily sexual on the part of the other person, but not for me. Once when I was playing on the schoolground a man exposed himself to me. But talking with my other women friends—straight, gay, and bi—almost with no exception they all had similar things happen to them. When I was about eleven some guy tried to drag me into his car while I was walking to dancing class.

"At the age of thirteen one of my distant cousins came to visit. What was important was I liked her. We'd romp around in bed, kissing and petting, but it still didn't connect as anything sexual. Whether or not it was deliberate, I'm not sure. But it was fun. She seemed to know what she was doing. The whole thing was ethereal. I didn't even remember it until several years ago. One day while I was making my bed and pulling the sheet up, this vision hit me. I realized, 'My God, when I was thirteen, Cindy and I played around in bed!' Before that it'd been a complete blank. I don't think I put it out of my head on purpose because it disturbed me, but rather because I felt it was so insignificant. It was one of those many childhood memories we forget and then some day remember. After I had that flash I saw my cousin and mentioned it to her. She said she didn't remember it. For her it was gone."

Disregarding the acts of aggression and those activities that had no sexual meanings for the women, 80 percent had their first sexual experience with a man.

Many women added qualifying statements to their answers. Because we are a nation that stresses heterosexuality, we think those relations are more "valid" than sexual expression between members of the same sex. Virginity is emphasized, and women are virgins until they have intercourse with a man. Comply, and you respond in accordance with societal dictates.

What were the circumstances surrounding that first time? The majority of the women—60 percent—were between the ages of sixteen and twenty. Thirty percent were fifteen or younger, and the remainder were twenty-one years old or older. All were single at the time, although some eventually married the man with whom they first had intercourse. Two-thirds of the women had older partners; one-third were the same age. The majority had intercourse with a long-term boyfriend rather than someone they had recently met.

Value judgments on motivations and feelings are difficult to translate into percentages, but some statements were made often enough to be included. Generally the women decided they wanted to shed their virginity. They wanted to find out what "sex was all about." After experimenting with many forms of sexual outlets without having intercourse, they thought the time had come. Some estimated they were passive, their partners being more aggressive during this initial time. Others felt they had been coerced by their boyfriends; some needed to rationalize what they were doing.

Sexual intercourse for the first time was not what it had been cracked up to be. Bells didn't ring; bombs didn't burst. Most evaluated this experience as unsatisfactory because of fear, nervousness, or their own lack of knowledge. Many women felt a psychological release from the "burden" of their virginity, but guilt followed.

The first love of Patricia's life lasted from when she was fifteen until she was twenty. They attended the same high school, held hands the way couples do, and experimented some. Eventually she wanted to carry things a little farther.

"My boyfriend wasn't really into sex, because he was

afraid of it. When I brought up the subject he'd call me promiscuous. We'd kiss, that was about the extent of his sexual passion. Finally, after what seemed years of discussion, we were going to have the big moment. We'd both seen enough B-grade movies to know what you were supposed to do. First you buy the bottle of booze, next the discomfort when you rent the motel room, and then . . . he couldn't get an erection. After nearly five years I was beginning to wonder if anything was ever going to happen. Since I wasn't too good at dealing with human emotions then, I asked him if he were ever able to get it up. As I recall, he stumbled out an evasive answer, 'Yeah, I think so. You don't have to worry about that.' I may not have had to worry, but he didn't come any closer to ending my virginity.

"He disappeared off to college and I went to visit him, even slept in the same bed with him, and he never touched me. By then I felt like screaming, 'Fuck this, I want to lose my virginity,' but somehow girls aren't supposed to do that. I wanted a resolution, so I set up a situation where I went to bed with someone else and ended up freaking out. I'd had a very proper Catholic upbringing, was in love with a guy who couldn't get it up, and there I was fucking somebody I didn't want to be with. It was very confusing for me, and I felt everything was closing in. Eventually I did pull my act together, but that first time was nothing I ever felt that good about."

Grace turned to her boyfriend, who had convinced her "it was a very natural thing" for them to do. Looking back to when she was sixteen, she said, "There's really not much to say because it wasn't all that unusual. No candles or incense, only the very uncomfortable back seat of his car. We'd become more and more daring. Finally I figured why not? I was pretty petrified about the whole thing. I remember now that it physically hurt, but not that much. It felt like what was actually happening—a little tearing, a little blood. What made it somewhat pleasurable was that I loved him very much. Accepting his warmth and being next to him was fantastic. Other sexual experiences with him were fine because he was always considerate and gentle."

Benetia viewed herself as the initiator. "After about a year-and-a-half of dating one guy and doing everything *but,* I decided it was about time. Seducing him wasn't my exact plan, but if I hadn't suggested it he probably wouldn't have pressed me. I'd discussed the idea in my own head, thought, 'let's do it,' and did. Afterwards I wanted to race out and holler, *'I fucked. Did anybody notice? Do I look any different?'* I really had fun, mostly because we knew each other's bodies so well anyway."

Peggy laughed when I asked about her first sexual experience. "Let me tell you about the quest to end my virginity. At nineteen I was absolutely ready to no longer be in that category. With all the press that sex gets, with all the dissuading I'd received from the church, I'd built up tremendous expectations about the moment. Bands obviously would start playing. Majorettes would twirl around the room. It was going to be something that would change my life! I'd been dating this guy who had to have more experience, because he certainly couldn't have had less. The scene was set, the curtain went up—and what a disappointment! I didn't even realize it had happened when it was already over. The guy asked, 'Well, do you feel different?' I answered, 'No, why should I?' So then he said, 'It's over.' *Over?* I didn't know we had completely started. Sigh. But now I realize I'd never masturbated. I had no idea of my sexuality. What could I possibly have expected to happen?"

Renée agreed. "It wasn't so magical. I was seeing this guy. Sexually we would do just about everything, but not actual penetration. Then one night I was supposed to go to a party and he wanted to see me before I went. He took me up to his house. I don't know if I surrendered or what, but I didn't want it to happen that night. I wanted to wait until I could spend more time with him. I had all those dreams. It hurt the first time, and I didn't enjoy it. The second time it hurt, too. By the third time it started getting better. I had expected it to be wonderful. Everything else had felt so good. I'd gotten so hot. I expected to work into it."

None of the women went into great detail about the first time they had intercourse. Amy explained, "All non-virgins know what it's like to make love to a man for the first time. If we want to educate our sisters, these first experiences are common bonds. But they are not different or unique for bisexual women."

Melanie was typical in that she did not speak about the specifics of the act. Instead she focused on the circumstances. "The first experience was with a man who was five years older than I. I married him later. As a matter of fact, he was the only one I went to bed with before I was married. It really happens, you know. We both felt it was compelled to happen. We had to. When I look back, it was definitely the reason I married him. Keep in mind this was fifteen years ago and we began living together, terribly secretively, for six months before we got married. I even kept the rent up on my room with my girl friend so our parents wouldn't know. Then I became pregnant and had an abortion, which locked me even more into 'us.' Fireworks did not go off that first time. The earth didn't move."

Judith, who was enrolled in a doctoral program at Harvard, was the oldest of three children. When she was twenty she had intercourse for the first time with a man ten years her senior. They ended up together for two reasons. "I was sick and tired of fooling around. I became involved with a man who was fighting being a homosexual. We had met at the time he was on the brink of suicide, and my savior complex came out. I put a lot of work and energy into him. He felt he'd fallen in love with me, which I think inherently I knew was not the case. But we did it. When it was over I thought, 'Is this it?' Nothing more, nothing less."

Jo summed up her feelings about sexual intercourse for the first time as "ho hum." "As far as actively going after a man and knowing what I was doing, that didn't happen until I was nineteen. Up until then I hadn't even officially petted with a guy. The high point of my sexual games was kissing and driving home. That very boring trip continued all through high school. But at the time sex simply didn't excite or interest me. For me there were more important things to do, so I didn't go through the feeling of wanting to get laid just for the sake of getting laid. If anything, I avoided it.

"When I finally got together with a man, I didn't particularly like it, but then I didn't start really enjoying sex until a few years ago. It was probably dissatisfying for the same reason most women discover. We don't know what pleases us and what doesn't. There are too many men who go under the illusion that all they have to do is stick themselves inside a woman and an explosion is going to occur. And it just doesn't happen. I had a long talk with a shrink about sexual gratification, and his first question was, 'Do you masturbate?' When I told him I'd never masturbated in my life, he said, 'Well godammit, go home and masturbate. Find out what you like about your own body.''

Twenty percent of the women defined their first sexual experience as being with another woman. Most were in their early teens, conscious decision was involved, and they acknowledged the sexual nature of the act. Generally these were situations in which a close friend spent the night and inquisitiveness led to exploration. There was mutual masturbation, sometimes including insertion of fingers in the vagina. Some of the women mentioned previously who had youthful experiences were not included in this percentage because they did not think of those activities in sexual terms. A few women mentioned they now recalled events from their childhoods where they related physically to another female, but until recently they had forgotten them.

One explained it this way. "When I was fifteen or sixteen my best girl friend and I stole a bottle of wine. After proceeding to get loaded, we had what I'd now consider my first sexual experience. At the time I didn't think of it in those terms because I thought it had to be with a man. Because her parents were gone we were spending the night together, and that's how it began.

"Masturbation was something totally new to me, but not to her. She showed me how to masturbate, and I think I brought her to orgasm. I fully knew it was not simple curiosity or something to share with a friend. It definitely had sexual connotations. Yet it was with another female. Society doesn't have the latitude to let you think of it that way consciously. We'd been friends for a long time, and I was always very close with my girl friends. Actually, when I think back I'm surprised I'd never done anything sexual before with any of them, because we were so united emotionally. In this first case I may not have been the initiator, but there certainly wasn't any reticence or hesitation on my part.

"It never happened again with that particular person, but that's not because I didn't want it to. It was in the summer and I had a job. The next morning when I went to work it was the old cliché—my heart was singing all day. I mean, it was the first sexual experience I'd had. It just so happens it was with a girl, but I was anxious to continue it. At the same time, I didn't have anything going with boys and she did. The feeling I got from her was that she was guilty about it. I don't know if that's true, but it never happened again."

In only a single case was there a hint of aggression in this experience of relating to another woman. But it was not a frightening occurrence. "I guess my first sexual experience was with another girl when I was about in the fourth grade," said Jackie. "There was an older girl in the neighborhood who must have been at least fourteen or fifteen. She locked me in a room, took off her clothes, and took me to bed with her. She told me things she wanted me to do, like kiss her breasts. I was probably intimidated by her, and that's one of the reasons I did it. Also, I was enjoying it."

Bisexual women did not by conscious decision immediately turn to another woman after their first intercourse with a man. For only 15 percent was the interval of time a year or less. Twenty-two percent did not have a relationship with a woman until two to three years had passed; 23 percent waited four to five years; 20 percent, six to seven years; and 20 percent did not act on any feeling of love they felt for members of the same sex until eight or more years had gone by.

The women became involved with other women for three basic reasons. Some said it was curiosity. They had seen, heard, and read about women loving women. Instead of relying on outside sources, they wanted to find out for themselves. Was it better, the same, different?—all the natural questions that people have about something they have not done themselves. They demanded first hand knowledge.

Others made the decision because they had always felt a strong bond between themselves and their female friends, yet they had never physically manifested it. "It was absurd not to carry love to a physical plane." Feminism and the women's movement were mentioned as giving them the courage not only to act on those emotions but also the supportive environment in which to do it. As they spent more time in the company of women and realized that competition for men's attention was meaningless, the warmth they felt for their sisters grew. But they still liked men.

The third reason cited was simplest. They "just happened to fall in love with a woman." Often the women were surprised. Prior to that they had been exclusively heterosexual.

For the majority, physically loving another woman that first time was satisfying, more so than their first experience with a man. But there were qualifiers. As Amy said, "Love's supposed to be better the second time around. Maybe making love with a woman for the first time is better for the same reasons." The women were older. Sex was no longer as much of a mystery. They knew more about themselves and their bodies. All of them had had intercourse with at least one man and so had personal reference for comparison. More thought was involved before going to bed with a member of the same sex. They realized they were breaking away from society's mold. For many, this first time was much more difficult to handle emotionally and intellectually than it had been when initially relating to a man. For some, a crisis situation occurred because of admission of being attracted to a woman. Often they would bombard themselves with questions about whether or not they had always been latent homosexuals. Was there something "wrong" with them? Others felt a whole new world had suddenly opened. They flowed with the exciting new experience.

The women believed it was more important to detail their thought processes before and after their beginning experience with women, feeling that to learn more about each other they must examine ideas as well as actions. They offered their stories to other bisexual women who feel alone. They wished to provide comfort and support, so no woman of this nature will feel isolated in her emotions.

Ann, now twenty-eight, was sixteen when she first had intercourse with a man. Two years later she turned to a woman. "That was my first year of college. I think it was the first experience with a woman for both of us, although we'd both been with men. Who initiated it wasn't a question; it just sort of happened. We'd been very close mentally and spiritually. There'd been some kissing, and we might have sat with our arms around each other on several occasions. Prior analysis wasn't part of it, because as far as I was concerned it simply welled out of the circumstances.

"You see, I'm exceptionally curious about the things I haven't done yet. What was important in this case was for the first time I *realized* I was attracted to women as well as men. Admiring women, noticing they were interesting, had always been there, but I'd never consciously focused on it or thought about it at all. My friend and I had totally different reactions afterwards, and perhaps one balanced out the other. She went into a period of being super-freaked out that she was gay. Maybe her going off the deep end mentally kept me anchored in an emotional calm, but I don't think I was ever heading in her direction. Mainly what happened for me was I became completely awestruck by female genitals. While I was investigating her body, learning and enjoying her, I kept thinking, 'It's like being inside me!' It was a mystical, beautiful, incredible experience. By being with her I felt I was uncovering parts of myself that had remained hidden. If nothing else, it made me even more curious to discover other levels of my being. I hadn't even masturbated before that."

Taylor is a vivacious woman who likes to do things that scare her. "I was nineteen when I first got it on with another woman. Neither of us knew what we were doing, but it was a mutual idea. She was older and more experienced. There were a lot of parallels to the time before when I was five years younger and had intercourse with a guy. But I was more in touch with my body, so I knew more of what was going on. It was more satisfying because there was more love at that time. This person I knew for a long time. We talked about it, and even though it scared both of us it also intrigued us. I always tell people you should definitely do things you're scared to do."

A combination of curiosity and practicing what she preached was the reason Stella went to bed with a woman. Beginning in high school and lasting several years after that, she had been in love with one man. When he went away to college she did not see as much of him, but they still talked about getting married some day. She had planned a trip to Central America, and the night before she left he came back from school to see her. "He told me he was bisexual. I couldn't relate to that at all. 'What does that mean, bisexual? I am a woman. I can take care of anything.' He said he felt he had to tell me."

In Guatemala Stella got a letter from him, outlining plans to join her. When they were together again, he talked about the problems of loving another man and the pressure he felt from society. She began listening as well as talking.

"By then I had gotten some distance and given it

some thought. I told him it didn't matter what sex you liked as long as you loved. But I was preaching that without living up to it. 'You're not hurting anybody,' I'd tell him. After so much talking on my part, going to gay bars with him, getting involved in the whole gay scene, I finally decided I'd better find out what it was all about. So I went to bed with a woman. Neither of us talked about it afterwards. I didn't say, 'OK, this is going to happen, so I want it to happen again.' It was just an experience. It was almost like being in bed with the second boy you ever knew."

That was three years ago. Stella has gone back and forth between men and women. For the past year she has been living with her female lover. When they became involved, it was no longer curiosity but a strong relationship.

For Gretchen the move toward relating to another woman was a slow process covering several years. During the progression of experiences, she paused to evaluate her feelings. "I had done a little experimenting with men and felt I knew what sex was about to some extent. One weekend I went with a girl friend to a house in the country. The two of us got completely stoned on dope and started playing some music that was very moving. It was one of those times when we were too stoned to talk, until suddenly she asked if she could touch my breast. With my degree of naïvete, I said, 'Why?' She explained, 'Every time I see you, you come on as a physical person. You hug and touch me. I think you're really a lesbian. I think you really want to . . . you know. . . .'

"Of course I figured what she was saying was she was turned on and she was the one who was the lesbian. The mind works in mysterious ways. But I didn't want to deny her, because she was a close friend. My own life told me there was nothing wrong with what she wanted to do. So I simply said, 'OK, you can.' She was sitting fairly far away from me, so she had to stretch her arm out and lean over to be nearer to me. She just touched my breast for a little while, but it was an emotional and strange, slow experience. Just as quietly these deep fears, these thoughts, were beginning to come out. First I thought, 'She's a lesbian!' Then as I started to breathe more deeply and become turned on, I thought, 'Oh, no, I am too!' Finally I guess my fears overwhelmed me, and I asked her to stop.

"I needed time to think about what had happened. As soon as the fear of the actual event had passed, which took quite a while, as soon as I had intellectualized it, I wanted to do it again. I wasn't afraid any more. I'd only required some space to evaluate the effect.

"About a year or two later I had my next experience with a woman, but through the back door. Let me explain that for me it wasn't really a 'relationship,' because it started when I was involved with a man. We'd invite another woman who was a mutual friend to join us in bed. We'd play with each other, explore, but usually the two of them would have intercourse and I'd feel it was my job to turn them both on. I didn't begin to consider that I might be bisexual until a couple of years later, after I was able to go to bed with a woman alone and have a good time. My feelings were basically, 'Well, I guess we're all bisexual. It depends on whether you ever have the opportunity to act on it or not.' It came down to my attitude that I'd always been this way, but hadn't thought of it.

"You see I didn't rush pell-mell into these feelings. After those few fumblings with women I knew I was no longer frightened, and curiosity began to take over. At that time I wasn't into exploring my own body, so by being with another woman I could grow in my knowledge of myself. Then I moved on to masturbation, and even now I'm totally hung up on it. I have to masturbate at least once a day no matter where I am. Just this summer I tried doing it on an airplane and in hot springs in the middle of the wilderness. I always wanted to do it in strange places, so it still may be my way of rebelling. My goal is to get to know my body and those of the people with whom I feel close."

Joyce is outgoing when the situation demands it but more withdrawn by nature. She calls herself a "realistic" artist—which means she has a part-time job as a waitress. Her hands are the first thing you notice, short, competent fingers—used to the work Joyce demands of them. As a teen-ager she had "been into men," but had always had many women friends. For her, the initial experience of loving a woman was not based on curiosity but on extending her emotions to another person. She considered the support and companionship were more important than the sexual side of their relationship. "I didn't find her particularly ravishing or attractive. I wasn't turned on to her physically because she had a nice body. In other words, my feelings weren't coming from her outward womanly characteristics. She seemed so pure, the original flower-child type, and that's the age in which it happened. I still remember she had on black-rimmed glasses, no make-up. She was wearing a trench coat. How dramatic! I couldn't forget her. It was as if she knew something. I thought about her, went by her house. I'd never even felt that way about a boyfriend.

"We first started out just rapping. This was the time when people were becoming loose. We'd sit down and talk about our souls—such a change from the fifties. It was an exciting time. Get stoned and experience new things and heights of sisterhood. The big thing was, we were sisters in spirit. I don't remember one specific occasion, one intimate explosion where we came together sexually. It started by holding hands. We'd snuggle, talk, and touch each other. This was all very gradual over a period of months. Finally she moved in with me. We'd kiss, then share the same bed. Sex was fine, but it wasn't the major issue. I loved her wise soul. We continued to relate to other people also. We never got jealous, because our love included room for other people.

"She was the first person ever to give me confidence in how I loved and how I touched people. She'd say, 'You're really warm. You're a beautiful person. You can love.' It was the first time anyone had told me I could love. Before that I didn't think I could show love, even though I felt it. It was a growing experience for me."

One woman, who is married and has a child, talked about the effect of the women's movement on her sexuality. "Women had always been the people I related to most easily, felt closest to, so feminism came easy to me. After I became involved with the women's movement I discovered—I don't know how to say it—it made me aware of the possibility of relating to women sexually. I didn't see it as a political statement or the 'politically correct' thing to do. But it lowered some of the emotional barricades for me.

"At that time I acknowledged to myself that I really did love one of my women friends. Although I'd always told her I loved her, it was then that I asked myself, and her, why I couldn't express my love physically. The mechanics of the situation were very involved because I'd been having an affair with her husband—which she didn't know about. She wasn't ready for a sexual relationship with another woman, she told me. I continued to see her husband, and in my mind that relationship became a symbolic one. In literature this is sometimes presented with two men sharing a woman rather than admitting or acting on their homosexual feelings for each other. By sleeping with her husband, I felt I had intellectually been manifesting my feelings of sexual attraction for her.

"In many ways she was my mother figure. She was several years older than I and had been through more 'domestic' experiences. She'd had kids, run her own home, and these were things she taught me how to incorporate into my life. But when it came to politics or new ideas it was always my dragging her along with me. After I revealed my feelings for her our relationship altered, and she began playing a role, doing things that I found extremely aggravating. When I'd go over to see her she'd get all dressed up and put on make-up, the whole bit. While she told me she couldn't fulfill anything sexually, she was teasing me with her actions. Our friendship fell apart for several months, but we eventually made love. It was pleasurable but not outstanding. She had a lot of sexual hang-ups in general. My subsequent relations with other women have been very good."

When Victoria was interviewed, she sat with her arms folded in front of her, her feet propped up on a hassock piled with papers. Organized chaos was the image she conveyed. Matching sweater and slack set, but with a safety pin to replace a missing button. Her hair looked as if it never needed combing—nor had it, for that matter. Victoria spent a great deal of time thinking through her philosophy of sexuality before she followed through on her beliefs. That conscious decision to be with a woman did not happen until she was twenty-eight. "Even prior to that age I'd acknowledged I'd been a woman-watcher, not a man-watcher, but I'd never really done anything. At a party or a restaurant when a lovely woman walked into the room, no matter how good-looking the man with her was, I always wound up staring at her. After countless discussions with some of my gay friends, I was still adamant that I had no intention of joining their ranks. I was very much attracted to men as well as women. It never dawned on me I could be bisexual. A further concern was society's attitude that if you had one homosexual experience you were obviously gay. It's as if with that single move you were declaring all of your past or future relations with men null and void. With the conditioning we're all exposed to, we learn there are only peaks and valleys. We have to get on one end of the pole or the other rather than shinny up and down.

"My feelings about women scared me in the beginning, because I felt society's pressure. Slowly some thoughts came to my mind, and this was prior to any heavy experiences with women. I decided anything I do on this earth I'd have to do because I wanted to and not because I was pressured into doing it by anyone else. If I were sleeping with both men and women because I wanted to, then that's where I was. I couldn't feel guilty about it. Also I think our sexuality is tied up with genetics, and there's certainly nothing I could do to change that.

"It's funny because suddenly I sensed a contentment with myself when I reached those conclusions. I even noticed I started man-watching a lot in addition to woman-watching. What the psychological context is I don't know, but it's worked well for me. Maybe it's always been a case of the bisexuality in me struggling to get out, saying, 'Hey, appreciate both men and women.' It's overkill, I suppose, like anything we do in life. Let me give you an example. If you get a little bit angry at someone about something and you don't air your views about it but hold them in, the day is going to come when you explode for some minor reason. By refusing to recognize my bisexuality for a long time, I went to the complete other extreme and convinced myself that if I ever slept with any woman at all, I was going to instantly turn into a lesbian. It was irrational. I feel I wasted a lot of years and the possibilities of good relationships by having that hang-up.

"After all that thought, I was completely ready for my first actual exploring with a woman. It took me a long time to get there, but when I did it was satisfying. The other woman hadn't gone through any extended period of introspection, and for her it was probably much more frightening. She was a complete closet case who was afraid of appearing as anything but exclusively straight. Because she was confused about her own feelings, she acted like someone in the movie *The Boys in the Band*. The next morning she greeted me with one of those lines, 'God, I was so drunk last night, what did I do?' From there I've gone on to good, solid relationships with both men and women."

Patricia sparkles when she talks. Her life hasn't been plagued by stunning emotional blows. This fact, she felt, contributed to her vibrancy. She's in perpetual motion—either coming from or going to some exotic location. Patricia exemplifies the woman who denied any bisexual feelings until she fell in love with one of her co-workers. Before that her memories included close girl friends in high school and college. She believed social mores kept her from examining her feelings at that time. Patricia's comments blended honesty and humor. "When in college I had a good friend that I spent a lot of time with. During that time we were both so uptight about what might have been going on between the two of us, so indoctrinated with socialization, that we couldn't and didn't live it out. To help her work through this dilemma, she began going to a psychiatrist. She actually told him she was afraid she was a lesbian because she felt so close to me, felt a strong desire to be with me. Then she related this to me, not in the sense of an invitation, but more along the lines of 'I have to get over this. This is what I told my shrink. This is what I'm messed up about.'

"We'd touch, touch hands, and I was aware of something but ignored it. We just didn't have enough courage or confidence in ourselves as people to just go ahead and do it. Then I got married and becoming involved with anyone else was not in my head. I've been brought up to believe you marry and that's the person you're with for life. My marriage ended for a variety of reasons, none of them having anything to do with sex. As a matter of fact, we had a great sexual relationship. After we separated and eventually divorced, I went through the typical reactions of sport-fucking, long-term affairs, brief interludes, but always with men. I had more time to think about myself and what I wanted out of life. Even though I knew I'd always liked women, had even had sexual feelings towards them, for some reason I'd never let myself go. The break, which was very gradual, came when I started working with a woman who'd been involved with other women. That was something different for me, and I was extremely curious.

"It wasn't one of those situations where love hit me over the head and we stomped off into the sunset. Over a six-month period I began asking her questions and started listening to what she was saying. It made a lot of sense. 'How can you say you don't love someone because of their genitals?' she'd ask me. 'What difference does that make? If you feel love for a person, want to touch her and be with her, why should you say no because that person has breasts instead of a penis?'

"I wanted to see where her head was, how she lived the way she lived. I started seeing just through my own childhood, how my bisexual leanings could have continued if it hadn't been for people telling me they were wrong.

"Probably at that point I began to think I could physically relate to another woman, but almost simultaneously the fear hit me, 'Oh, my God, am I a lesbian? How awful! Am I sick?' Yet my feelings of attraction for men hadn't suddenly disappeared. The mental gymnastics disturbed me, because I hadn't achieved the plateau of a middle ground. You have to be one way or the other—gay or straight—I thought.

"I felt in my heart that my love for this one person was developing. Also, I knew if I allowed myself to experience her sexually, it wasn't going to be the kind of relationship where you can sleep with somebody and then walk away. But that was the way I usually felt about men as well. Sometimes there are people I feel a tremendous attraction for, a soulhood almost. I know if I get involved it will be very intense. There are other times I become interested but I sense it'll be lighter, maybe mellower, maybe overnight, a week. With others it's almost a possession I get. My concern would have been as great if she'd been a man, because it had to be a conscious choice.

"One night when we were talking in the car she put her arm around me and touched me in a certain way that I hadn't been touched by a woman before. She said, 'I want to get to know you this way.' I didn't say anything. Another month went by before anything else happened. It took six months to live this whole thing out. It took six months for me to work out loving a woman. Everybody takes the time they need.

"Finally we had work to do outside the city, which meant we spent the night in the same bed. She'd try to snuggle up, but I'd just laugh and say, 'Oh, no, sleep on your side of the bed. Don't touch me.' At the end we were sleeping hugging each other. Then about a week later we began a month-long trip. One night I rolled over, kissed her, and it started. So far our love has lasted over a year.

"It was a conscious decision, and once I made up my mind by telling myself I wasn't crazy, it was all right. I'd counsel myself, 'You're not a freak. You're just like everybody else, and you feel love for this person. You're a physical being who likes touching people. Go ahead, and whatever consequences you feel as a result, deal with them when they happen.'

"Who knows, we could have touched each other and gone blah, but I didn't think that would happen, because I knew my love and desire for her. I touched her that way. And it was fabulous, really gratifying. I didn't have an orgasm the first time, but not too long after that.

"Even over this past year I've continued to relate to men. I started actually calling myself bisexual when I'd finally extended my feelings of love from a woman to the physical level. How could this decision bother me; it was so very natural. I mean, I didn't get warts on my fingers or anything. I didn't feel weird about it.

"To me it doesn't matter if I'm dealing with a male or female. I know I'm feeling these things because suddenly I'm aware of my body sensations. When the actual sexual performance enters the picture, I believe I'm doing things from instinct rather than choice. The element of selection comes before, when you decide whether you're going to be with a specific person— male or female is inconsequential. By adding that previous idea of choice, you can bring about bisexuality. Other times I'm convinced everyone's bisexual but society tries to keep an orderly garden. No stragglers or weeds in the neat rows of sexuality.

"It's obvious from my own childhood that I was or am bisexual, and I know it. If socialization, the media, and the church hadn't leapt in, I probably wouldn't have muted those desires in myself for so long. You choose friends of both sexes when you're a child, but when you become an adult you have to limit yourself from total knowledge of a person because of gender. Discrimination is valid and I don't recommend hopping from bed to bed, but a decision should be based on emotions, not sexual differences."

Patricia, as well as the other women interviewed, did not race out to convince friends that bisexuality was the only and best game in town. She believed this sexual orientation was preferable for her.

When and why the women defined themselves as bisexual was an individual matter. The time and circumstances varied from person to person. They did not recite a place, date, or moment, but presented a growing awareness. Sometimes a philosophy came first. The women acknowledged the possibility of physically relating to a woman before acting on those emotions. For some, such as Patricia, the decision came after the fact, after they had gone to bed with a woman—and enjoyed it. Approximately 20 percent said they disliked all labels. They were willing to be interviewed because they met the "requirements," but they had chosen this lifestyle because they refused to be shoved by society into a gay or straight category.

Maria said, "If I must have a label call me pansexual, ambisexual, antisexual, adrogynous, neutral, undecided . . . just don't make me into something I'm not!" Joyce suggested a more rational way of viewing all sexual acts. "Why not use the words heterosexual and homosexual as adjectives instead of nouns? Maybe you're doing a thing with some man. At that moment it is a straight experience. That doesn't mean you're exclusively straight. Later you might be getting it on with a woman. For that time and space you're involved in a lesbian relationship. That doesn't mean you're going to be gay or straight forever. Can't we ever learn to give each other some room to maneuver?"

Cindy is twenty-two and has a bachelor's degree in English. Six months after her first experience with a woman, she began to view herself as bisexual. Several of her close friends were bisexual, and she felt this supportive environment helped her. "I had felt the possibility of being able to love men and women as early as high school, but I don't know if it was a conscious understanding of what that would involve. After I'd been intimate with both sexes, it felt right. I can't go by society's conventions and what's accepted, because a lot of times it just doesn't feel right. Loving men and women felt good to me. It wasn't screwing me up. It wasn't creating any problems. It wasn't having to make a choice; no one pressured me toward one sex or the other. I had an outside environment that was open to my needs and an understanding of myself. This is where I'm at. This is OK. As simple as that."

Belief in her bisexuality came before the reality for Renée. "I'd been spending my whole life saying I'm bisexual. I can't see closing myself off to other possibilities. Finally I did something about it, and it seemed positive. Then for a time I cut off all sexuality. Sex in general bothered me, so I stayed away from everyone. I couldn't initiate or make love to anyone. I needed somebody to make love to me. I thought getting fat would prevent me from being in sexual situations. People seemed to be having sex without assuming any responsibility for each other's emotions. And that's wrong. Now I've come full circle. Bisexuality makes more sense to me than being gay or straight. I can't see cutting off a relationship with a person anywhere. How can you say I've known you *this* far, but I won't know you any farther because you're the same sex? I learn from everybody I meet."

Maria didn't mince words as she talked about defining her sexuality and sex role stereotypes. "For a long time I bought that deal about there being masculine and feminine, heterosexual and homosexual. But it freaked me out. I had to do it, yet it was like a dog chasing its tail. It caused tension in me and was part of my crazies. I hate to be stereotyped in anything. When I say I'm bisexual I'm saying I'm not going to stereotype myself into having to be one thing or the other. I'm talking about being bisexual not in terms of sexuality but in terms of anything. Antisexual is pretty much how I feel, and it's the word I like to use.

"Now I feel totally integrated, with separate components. What I see is that I'm me. I do what I want to do. I dress however I feel like dressing. My interests are whatever they are. Those people out there who go, 'Well, that's female, that's male . . .' they're the ones who are putting the labels on the acts. They're the ones who're dividing everything into two groups. It's not me. I'm one and the same. My self-image is androgynous.

"It wasn't easy for me to come to these conclusions. First I had to learn a lot about myself. I had to get it on with men. I had to discover a woman and play the usual head trips on myself. 'I'm a dyke. I'm queer. I'm despicable.' But I got through that, and I didn't have leprosy. Then it took a fine relationship with an exclusively gay woman to bring me along further. We both went through changes, but at the same time I kept seeing all those real truckdriver women at the gay bars—in the valley of the dykes. Jesus, can you imagine what it's like to go around in black leather jackets, hunched backs, drinking beer?

"I've chosen to be 'bisexual' for some very simple reasons. Women are sexy. Men you can fuck. I'm not ready to give up either. I'm not even willing to settle down. I've got straight, gay, and asexual relationships going right now, and I like them just fine. For me sexuality is a function of mental health and participation, not a function of gender."

Fran, who is in her thirties, took a longer time to resolve her conflicts about her sexual orientation. She is married, but it is not an exclusive relationship. When having an affair with a woman, which threatened her marriage, she saw a notice for a bisexual rap group. She attended, and that and later meetings aided her in clarifying her self-image. "I realized because of the abrupt collision of those two worlds that I'd always kept so separate—my supposedly gay feelings and my public heterosexual self—that I couldn't very well do that any more. I had to look at my sexuality. That's how I started, through looking at it with other women who were somewhat in the same situation I was.

"Being in the group has helped me tremendously. The one thing it's done is given a sort of legitimacy to my own feelings. In an internal sense I'm not crazy. Other people have experienced this too. It's not uncommon, which is what everyone likes to say about bisexual women. They'll come out with, 'You're just in transition. Wait awhile and you'll be on one side or the other.' Most of the women in my rap group expressed the belief that they see this as a viable lifestyle. What that has meant for me has also been in terms of the people I relate to sexually. I've learned to be very upfront about the aspect of commitment, time, and the investment of energy. I try to be very clear about the limitations I place on relationships outside my marriage. This is something that all people who're involved in a permanent but open relationship should do. It took the group to help me see that. Just being with other women—many were married, too—made me feel stronger and better about myself. When you know you're not alone, you can handle things better."

Alicia was not as lucky. She still felt isolated in her feelings because of lack of support. "Ever since seventh grade I've been aware I was attracted to both sexes. That's been the major traumatic issue all my life. It's caused lots of confusion. It's something I feel I have to keep inside me. Something I can't talk to anyone about."

These were the exceptions. Most of the women interviewed were comfortable with their sexual life-styles.

Any emotional conflicts they had felt were now in perspective. They had been more introspective about the choices they were making because they were charging the waves of society's conditioning. It is rarely easy to be different, especially in a nation which puts such a high premium on heterosexuality. But they were content. Their attitude is that if the public is disconcerted by bisexual women, then the national attitudes need re-ordering—there is no reason for them to change.

4.

Passion
and Propriety

Ask any random group of exclusively heterosexual women what characteristics attract them in men, and you get replies as diverse as those from bisexual women. Apply the question to lesbian women about physical attractions to members of the same sex, and the results are similar. Some emphasize bodies, others minds, spirituality—or a combination of qualities. The difference for bisexual women is what they do about that attraction. Being sexually interested in a man is deemed natural by our standards. Physically manifesting that feeling for a woman is not. All women know the rules for acting on their desires to be with a man, but when dealing with a woman whose sexual orientation is unknown, the field is uncharted.

It is easy to get a percentage breakdown of answers to the question, "Were you first sexually attracted to men, women or both?" But it is difficult to tabulate emotions, philosophies, and specific qualities of attraction. Therefore, while the data revealed that 55 percent of the women originally felt physical attraction for both sexes, 25 percent primarily for men and 20 percent for women, the responses basically involve preference for individuals rather than gender. As Claire pointed out, "How can you give point values to similarities and differences in attractions to men versus women when each time you fully interact with a person the coupling assumes its own dimensions?"

Numbers and fractions can be carried to absurdity. Does it matter that nearly 60 percent of the respondents stated they have strong breast fetishes, or that 95 percent feel the color of a man's eyes makes no difference to them? The relevant information is more complex. For each of the following questions I selected five women's answers. I chose some who were representative of many women, and others who voiced their ideas more succinctly, went into greater detail, or gave an individual slant. They present a perspective on the similarities and differences of sexual preferences among bisexual women.

QUESTION: What characteristics are you attracted to in men and women, and are they similar or different?

BENETIA: One of Benetia's main concerns is fighting a battle with weight. She's exercising as often as possible, passing up her favorite desserts. Her all-American looks are accentuated by a small, aquiline nose, wide eyes, and a slight sprinkle of freckles across her cheeks. She is a politically oriented feminist but feels that does not mean by definition that she must look drab. Her closet is filled with a bright array of halter tops, jeans, long-skirts, and chic blouses. There's a charm about her that is contagious. She is talkative and did not mind the personal nature of the questions, because she firmly believes that bisexual women should be better comprehended by the general public.

"I think I'm more attracted to women after I get to know them and feel a certain rapport. With men, it can be an immediate attraction because of the way they look. Every now and then this can be an instant thing—just seeing them on the street or at a meeting. But you know, that may all be due to social mores and pressure. I mean, if I see a man I'm attracted to, even if I don't know him well, I can tell him I'd like to go to bed with him. But I obviously can't approach a woman without knowing something about her sexuality or whether my expression of feelings would ruin our friendship. So I may repress attractions I feel, knowing I can't act on them.

"Just imagine I'm at a party. I notice this woman who really fascinates me. I can't breeze up to her and say 'Hey, I'm attracted to you. Let's go to bed!' Much more groundwork has to be done. I have to know a woman better before anything might eventually happen. Determining whether I experience interest on the part of the other person enters into it, but this is more true for women than men. The trouble is, I'm impatient. I hate to wait for the other person—male or female— to get it together to start something.

"A couple of weeks ago I told a friend of mine that I was going to be interviewed for a book on bisexual women. She was really amazed. I have a husband and kids, so to all intents and purposes it looks as though I'm heterosexual. I guess that's why she was so surprised. We've always been friends, though not extremely close, but ever since she found out I am bisexual she's been flirting with me. But when we talk about the subject of women loving women, she says she just can't understand it. She's definitely intrigued, but I can't deal with this kind of situation. I'm very inhibited about beginning relationships with women, because often you have to go through so much shit that I'd rather wait and see if they'll make an overture. It's funny, because I'm aggressive with men.

"What I'm attracted to and excited by in men and women are their differences. I like women because they are soft and smooth. I like men because they're rough-skinned and hairy. I'm being honest. I know I'm laughing and it sounds ridiculous, but it's the truth. Also I'm going to open myself up to shrieks when I tell you I'm attracted to people who admire me. There goes my self-image out the window. I'm just an ego-maniac!"

MERLIN: The older of two children, Merlin was raised in New York. Her father, a businessman, was frequently absent from home. When there, he was indulgent and supportive, but she fought with her mother. At sixteen Merlin had intercourse with a man. Six years later she physically related to another woman for the first time. She is a lean-boned, fragile person with blond, shoulder-length hair. In school she might have been the beauty queen runner-up, lovely but not stunning. Yet she would resent that comparison, because, as a feminist, she does not want any woman to be treated as an object. She did not hedge my questions but answered them directly, leaving room for interpretation.

"There are similarities and differences in what I'm attracted to in women as opposed to what I look for in men. Each person I meet I approach as an individual entity. I'm attracted to my visual opposites, and that's true for both sexes. I'm not turned on by blond, blue-eyed men or women. That's what I look like. I want someone who isn't a carbon copy of myself.

"I stay away from the extreme in women—I don't go for the super-butch types who fashion themselves as truckdrivers. But that doesn't rule out the fact that I notice women with certain masculine qualities or who dress in a masculine, or perhaps neuter way. The other day I saw this incredible lady riding down the street on one of those enormous motorcycles. She had long, straight, black hair and no make-up. She looked as if she could be male or female. To me she was beautiful, not only in physical appearance but in the strength she represented as well. Also, I've got to admit I've got that American hang-up about breasts. Needless to say, I'm really flat-chested and maybe it's the opposite attracts theory at work once more.

"Then there are men. For awhile I've been leaning toward black men. The reasons for this are unclear to me, but I'm just functioning instead of wondering about them. I think it's first the physical thing, and with black men I'm just interested in the differences in the body, the skin, and a certain air of self-confidence. The eyes are very important to me. A man has to be sensitive and intelligent. I could fuck some guy once that I thought had a really nice body and was appealing, but if when he opened his mouth he blew it, I couldn't get into it again."

GRACE: Being around Grace is like coming in contact with an exposed high-tension wire. She exudes sparks, energy, and life. She tells me her friends feel exhausted after spending a day with her. Every minute is planned and programmed with activity. There is no wasted motion. Her appearance is practical. Short, close-cropped auburn hair, hazel eyes, chunky build. She dresses for convenience in her standard "uniforms," which she alternates for a span of a few months before tiring of them and venturing out with some new combination. Her mother died several years ago, but she maintains contact with her father. Nine years ago, at the age of twenty-two, she began defining herself as bisexual.

"My sense of attraction to people has changed over the years. Men and women answer a different set of needs for me, but I'm not necessarily attracted by different things according to the sex of the person. The physical is important, but not just physical beauty. I tend *not* to like people who are conventionally beautiful. By that I mean your standard, garden variety American ideal of manly or womanly beauty. I can experience their beauty, but it doesn't make me want to go near them. Basically I like hard men and soft women. Soft men drive me up the wall. I like gentle, sensitive men, so it's a different kind of use of the word 'soft.' It's like a rare breed. I'm talking about men who have direction, know where they're going in life, but allow you and themselves the freedom to cry, sigh, and be whoever you want to be.

"My attraction lately is very heavily mental. When I was younger it relied on the physical. I was attracted to someone at the moment. But now I really wait until

I know that person's mind. Because it just doesn't work until then. Sometimes I don't feel interested in either sex. I get a lot more satisfaction from masturbating, since I don't need to go to bed with another individual for any kind of release. No, ladies and gentlemen, all bisexual women are not raving sexual beings who continually thirst for hedonistic pleasures.

"I'm a Virgo and we're supposed to be very attracted to Capricorn men. That's proven to be a fact with me. I feel a great deal of empathy and real comfort with other Virgos of both sexes. Currently there're three Aries who are important to me, but our relationships aren't always easy. We don't seem to understand each other immediately. I have to be very clear, very careful. I brush aside gender differences and try to get inside the person's head. That's the important part of any attraction or eventual relationship."

RAMONA: There are three children in Ramona's family. Her early years were spent in southern California and then in San Antonio, Texas. After graduating from college she left San Antonio, frustrated by the prejudice against her Chicano background. Originally she was embarrassed by her heritage, but now she is proud of it. She can readily switch between Spanish and English midway through a sentence. That double fluency was instrumental in her employment as a teacher of English as a second language.

When she answered my questions there were pauses, regressions, silences, and smiles. At the end of the interview she opened a bottle of wine and said, "I feel that I've just had a session with a shrink. Most of these questions I'd never thought about. I'm glad now that I did."

"My attraction to men and women . . . let me think. All my life I've been very close to women, and it didn't matter at all what they looked like. And it always did make a difference to some extent what the men's outward appearance was. If I was going to date him, he had to be 'cute.' If he was cute, it was cool.

But with women, as I said, it didn't enter into my choice of them as friends or lovers. If I cared for them I did because of who they were inside, not how they appeared outside. Now that I'm getting older, I try to work past exterior values for men and look at their souls as well.

"Sometimes I believe I'm attracted to that intangible quality called 'sexual vibes' or 'energy' that an individual might be giving off. Is there a spark, a flash, a small sonic boom? With some people it's a physical thing, others more spiritual. It's hard to say in my own mind which is first, or whether they go hand in hand. My intellect tells me there should be no difference, but I'm unclear."

MARIA: Maria, who was described in Chapter 2, received her introduction to male/female sex at nineteen. A few years later she turned to women as well.

"What attracts me to people is their bodies. My mother was an artist of sorts and influenced me in this way—to notice what is beautiful and why it's beautiful. There're certain body types I like in men and certain ones in women. But sometimes I have relationships with body types that have little resemblance to my ideal. At this point in my life I'm also looking for emotional involvement. Before it might have been more what they looked like. Let's put it this way, I'm totally inconsistent.

"Now the wrinkle comes when I want to do something. I'm a lot better at initiating sex with men, because women can be really tricky. I've had many relationships with women where there were definite sexual undertones. I could see it. I don't know whether I've X-ray vision or I'm better at reading signs in other people's behavior, but I'm aware. There've been numerous women who were practically writing out to me, 'I'm sexually turned on by you. Let's do something about it!' And so when some woman comes to me with this ball, I pick it up and go 'Great! Far out!' and I throw it back at them. Then they go 'What ball?! What're you doing? I don't understand!' There's the rub; that's the difference. Men you like, and you say let's get it on. Women you like, and you have to get wrapped into all kinds of fancy footwork games before you can get down to some fun."

Why people end up in bed together is a mystery. What is known is whether the end result was first based on friendship or an immediate attraction. Thirty-two percent said their relationships with both sexes begin as friendships then move on to the sexual level. The time element can be short, but there is a definite companionship developed prior to any sexual involvement. Twenty-eight percent replied it is generally an instant interest on their part. They see a person, male or female, and the attraction is immediate. The remaining 40 percent? These women acknowledge a distinct difference in how their relationships begin with women and with men. When they eventually make love with another woman, it is within the framework of friendship. They meet, talk, exchange ideas, and a commonality of feelings grows between them. Later the emotions carry to a physical plane. With men the reverse takes place. They go to bed and afterwards learn more about each other's minds.

Bisexual women erase the demarcation between the sexes, perceiving men and women as individuals. They say that loving both sexes helps them learn more about themselves. After the inherent confusion involved in recognizing the possibility of relating platonically and sexually to every adult they meet, they see this as a self-liberating experience. But differences in their sexual/love relationships become apparent. While the majority stress the person, the particular individual, many observe that differing needs, wants, and expectations are answered by men and by women.

This suggests another question. If one prefers or finds greater satisfaction with one gender, why continue to relate sexually to the other sex? Doris summed up the response for the entire group with this analogy:

"To me that question is ridiculous. I like both strawberry and chocolate ice cream. Just because I like certain things about strawberry, it doesn't mean I'm going to stop sampling chocolate. It's still good—just in a different way. Sometimes I have a craving for one, then I prefer the other. The same holds true for men and women." Obviously, loving someone and having sex with someone can be two different experiences. Because I worded the question broadly, the women answered with greater leeway.

QUESTION: On a sexual/love basis, do you find men or women more satisfying, equally satisfying, or satisfying in different ways?

ELAINE: Elaine is a thirty-five-year-old divorcee. After receiving her B.S. degree from the University of Chicago, she held several different jobs. For the past three years she has been working as a sex therapist, mainly with women clients. She comes from a middle-class family and has one brother, ten years older. At seventeen she became involved with a man, at twenty-seven with a woman. She married at age eighteen and divorced five years later. For the last five years she has been living with a bisexual man in a non-monogamous relationship. Her two children, ages seven and nine, spend the summers with Elaine and the winters with their father.

"I definitely think that men and women are sexually satisfying in different ways. This isn't because of purely physical differences but the way they view sex itself. My experiences as a therapist show me that men need relationships as much if not more than women. Women are brought up with an accepting idea about sex. 'Yes, we're going to do it. Every woman does.' Women are no longer so uptight about their sexuality. They can think about sex. They can think about masturbation. And they can act or not act on it. Men get into this thing about performance. They get into being a critic. Men become so concerned about specifics—like how long they fuck—that they don't get into pleasurable lovemaking.

"For them it all boils down to performance. They don't get into the moment itself. By the time they start screwing, they're already done. They've scored. They're somewhere else as opposed to being right there. Sex is not something they can think about. It becomes only something they can react to. Very rarely can they talk or relax about it, because they have all these images going around in their heads about Don Juan, Harry Reems—all of which is real straight fucking. They don't place much emphasis on sensuality or experimentation. I guess that sort of codifies it—women are able to experiment, whereas men aren't.

"The thing I like about women is they're understanding. They'll listen to you talk. They can usually identify with the types of experiences I'm talking about —which is sort of feeling unsure of myself and what I'm doing. I may know what I want, but I may not know how to go about it. Women identify. Men put you down. They don't want to hear about that. That's one of the things I really relate to about women. They just seem to be much more compassionate to me than men. I feel friendly with women. I find it very hard to feel friendly with men. I find that most of the time there's a competitiveness with men, which I don't like.

"What turns me on with both men and women is being made to feel good about myself. When anybody relates to me in a way that makes me feel comfortable with myself, that's great. Men very often find me challenging, even though I don't mean to be. I don't put that across. My interpretation is I have to do sex therapy when I deal with men. I've a lot of sexual information, because I taught sex education before my current job. I've always been interested in sexual growth. Most men find that threatening. They feel they're going to get rated or something. They're concerned I'm not going to deal with them as people. But women tend to be curious, and when I start talking to them they find out that indeed they can get into talking about sex. Everybody is basically pretty anxious about their performance and how they're doing. Women usually feel pretty much at ease, and I feel the same. We do talk about sex.

"In general it's admiration that turns a person on. Unfortunately men admire me for all the wrong reasons —because I have a nice body, because they think I'm going to be a stud. The more a man gives me masculine attributes, the more it turns me off. I like to be touched, but I have a real hard time initiating sexual contact. I have to really want to have sex, but I feel very hesitant about touching the other person. I'm trying to get over that. After that initial touch I usually feel secure with the entire situation and nothing really fazes me. I can get into it.

"I find it easier to initiate sex verbally with women than with men. Women will be submissive. Women will let me touch and pleasure them. Men often have a hard time letting me do what I want with them. I find more of a give-and-take with women. Although I also see that women very often will be passive and let me make love to them. They'll let me go down on them and give them orgasms and very frequently won't reciprocate. Men reciprocate almost too much. I feel overwhelmed. There really does have to be some medium ground. Both men and women are important to me. I haven't given up men, but at this precise moment I have a slight preference for women. Who knows what next month will bring."

RENÉE: During the last seven years Renée has been an on-again-off-again student. Because she has been supporting herself since she was nineteen, she has had to periodically drop out of school to work. At the time of her interview she was back at school while holding down a part-time job. Her favorite course is in women's studies. Between classes and work, she participates in a theater group. Although her childhood was spent in New Jersey, Renée has moved four times during the last several years. Her manner is frank and direct. The intensity she feels about many subjects is reinforced by her physical characteristics. Sweeping gestures, expressive violet eyes, rapid speech. Every movement, every furrow of her brow has a purpose.

"There must me differences because I feel the union between a man and a woman is a different power than that between two women. Between a man and woman there are unique things to consider—magical power, I guess. It's more the design of the universe. When the question of reproduction enters into a relationship you must deal with that power, and it's much more intense. That's not to say sleeping with a strange man is more valid than with a close woman friend, it's just a totally different kind of force. When you sleep with a woman it's a pleasurable, giving, soft flow. It doesn't have to be, but that's usually been my experience. Making love to a woman is like making love to myself. The goddess idea enters into it. A total acceptance of my womanness. When I'm making love to a man, ideally maybe the female principle and the male principle are trying to unify, trying to come together. I believe that's a cosmic thing. In many ways making love to my sisters is helping me unify the male and female in myself.

"It's easier in a lot of respects to make love to another woman. We seem to understand each other. We don't have to put on any special airs. I feel I don't always have to look like a fashion model to make love to a woman, but with men sometimes, the average, straight man, I think there's that expectation on their part. We don't have to be glamorous before loving men either, but somehow it seems that I feel a pressure to. I have had a great many men and women friends in my life, but I've made love to more men. I feel I'm less open with men. I guess that's my problem, though.

"Lately I've been thinking I'd like to have a perfect union with a man, just because I think it's on a higher plane. I know I can have as near a perfect union with a woman just because my solidarity with my sisters is there. Add sex to my relationships with women and the basic emotions are unaltered. With men, when you add sex there are changes.

"The kind of men I've been making love to recently have been bisexual. I believe people who're bisexual are more willing to explore. They're not into 'I'm a man and you're a woman, honey.' They just want to make you feel good and feel good themselves. And they understand the nature of sexual experiencing. I've been sleeping with men who are gay or haven't slept with a woman in years. I find they're more willing to get close. With many straight men there's a bubble—they're in their bubble and I'm in mine. I'm fighting furiously to get out of mine and into theirs or bring them into my bubble—or just have a joint bubble. But my God, it's hard with most straight men.

"When I'm with a woman it's more just wanting to hug, cuddle, kiss, and make love. Women seem to have more a smoldering love; with men, it's more of a burning. When I'm enjoying a woman it's just an expression of my love for her. I love the kind of spirit we have together that I've never felt with a man. More, less, equal satisfaction? It's all of the above."

JUDITH: Judith is of Arabic descent. At twenty-eight years of age she is a beautiful woman spiritually as well as physically. The day I interviewed her she was in the midst of moving from one apartment to another. While packing boxes, she said she did not think about her sexuality. She shies away from all labels. She has loved individual men and individual women, but since she has become involved with the women's movement, intellectually her ties are stronger with women. Her feminist beliefs have strained some of her relationships with men.

"There's no question in my mind that men and women are satisfying in different ways. At times I've been disappointed by men, other times the women were not enjoyable. When I've been dissatisfied, it's because of the reasons behind getting together. Sometimes I need sex. I'll go to a bar, pick someone up and go home with them to relieve what I consider to be pent-up frustrations. Recently that happened with a man. The sex we had was physically good, but I know in my head I was bored, even though he was doing everything possible to make it pleasurable for me as well as himself. That's unusual in itself. But I wasn't totally attracted to him. I didn't feel that 'thing,' so I couldn't respond. After that the same thing happened with a woman. Sex, but not complete enjoyment.

"My relationships with women in general have been good. Somehow in my mind there's no threat of anything when I think about going to bed with a woman. I feel there's been more honesty in my sexual relationships with them than with men. My sexual dealings with men have been strained because a lot of them are threatened by me. In the first place, I'm not a dumbie and I won't act like one. In the second place, I feel that having myself together as a person, a woman, and liking it, is very frightening to a man. There's no way I'd want to be a man. I've always felt that. My life is very centered around being female; and that also intimidates many men.

"My sexuality is disturbing to some men who are very heavily macho types. I never think twice about being the aggressor if that's the way I feel. Most men don't like that at all. I've met very few who can accept it as a part of my own sexuality. I'm not going to be passive and say, 'Oh, isn't this nice. Thank you.' What a bore!

"I find women's bodies much more beautiful than men's. I really enjoy the fact women have breasts. I like the intimacies of touching women and having them allow themselves to be cuddled and caressed. Men are less prone to want that kind of thing. With men I really like the physical side of sex, which is much stronger with them than with women. I mean that in terms of using your body more. I also like the feeling of having a man's penis inside me. Sex with a man or woman can be a wonderful thing. My mental feelings toward the individual are what makes the difference."

LIZ: Liz often characterizes her life in terms of numbers. The oldest of three children, she was from an upwardly mobile family in New Mexico. She first had sex with a man at the age of sixteen and was thirty before she became physically intimate with any woman. During that span of years she had two husbands, three abortions, and more jobs than she cared to talk about. But her primary interest has always been films. After receiving her master's degree from the University of Michigan, she headed to New York. There were several more stops along the way before she ended up on the West Coast. She is now a free-lance film-maker.

"I feel it's important to examine love relationships before zeroing in on the sexual aspect. First let me say I'm not attracted to people in general. I become interested in those who have stamina and creativity. I look for a sense of humor. I want them to have some sort of goal that relates to something other than money or working for Standard Oil. We must contribute in some fashion, so I guess I look for people who do that. I like people who to me are aesthetically pleasing, not mediocre looking. And I like people with style. When you set up those qualifications you can go screwing around, and I certainly did that, but now I'm talking about similarities and differences in loving a male or female versus merely fucking an individual.

"I've certainly had a varied sex life. It's included a catastrophic liaison with a friend of my father's which played out some kind of nightmare game between my father, this man, and me. I was involved with a whole group of theater people, then marriage, a divorce, an affair with a married man—which was a grotesque, devastating mind fuck—on down to fine, loving attachments. I think what I'm doing is setting up a series of experiences to support my theories.

"My opinion has to do with the ways in which people love each other. Women tend to treat their love for each other as trivial—feeling because they're both women they're liberated if they can love each other to start with. But because the person they love is another woman, it's not as important as loving a man. That reflects back on them, too. It means they're not taking themselves as seriously as they should; thus they're not taking their relationship with another woman as seriously as they should. From my experiences with men and women there literally should be no differences between the quality of love. It is a love relationship, but I keep seeing women brushing off their relationships with other women.

"I think there's so much ambiguity and ambivalence in themselves. Two women in this culture who love each other sometimes seek ways to sabotage their relationship. They don't seem to give the other woman as much value or worth as they might a man. They think loving a woman is bad. That's what we're brought up to believe. 'There must be something wrong with me if I love this woman, therefore I'll set up these little circumstances to hurt me, her, and the relationship because I've done this dreadful thing.'

"I believe the anguish that I see in this country stems from the fact we're never even taught to love well in the accepted relationships of male/female. When you step outside that, you confront all of the other problems you have in any relationship with an overlay of social mystique. That's very painful and almost demented, suicidal in a sense. There are rare exceptions, two people finding each other and staying together. They work out all the problems and really get to know each other, improve, help one another. I don't think that anyone until they're in their thirties can get enough lead time on their own experiences to see what they're doing to themselves or to other people, or how they can improve in order to have a happier life. We don't seem to place any great value on a lot in this country, and it distresses me. We feel that we *ought* to be happy, and we go around desperately seeking ways to be contented. I know I have, to the detriment of my work and psyche. We feel we *ought* to be successful. We feel we *ought* to be rich and comfortable. And once you look at these values they seem very, very shallow. I know that isn't a sexual philosophy, but sex is just completely intertwined with affection and with your own feelings about yourself. You can't separate them.

"Sex just for its own sake with a man or a woman— what a question. You see I never really enjoyed sex with anyone for a great number of years. Again, it goes back to my theory that we're not taught anything. Women should stick to older people for their first sexual experience. Preferably a kind one, get some instruction. There ought to be a sense of responsibility that those older people feel. For me, sex with a woman is very comfortable, because I don't have to pretend. There can be a real sharing and a real sense of equality in that relationship. But it can be just as tough and as much work as a relationship with a man. It's not different in that way. Some people may think it is, or some may believe it's more tantalizing. *I* don't think it is, if you really love the individual as a person. Now if you're just loving women for women, that's something else. But I love for people. I've learned to recognize my own sexuality after being with women. I *like* loving women. And I *like* loving men. The uniqueness comes with the individual, not the sex of the person. It's just that you've got to take care of yourself."

MARIA: I selected Maria's response to this question as well as the previous one because she speaks with candor and humor, and for many women.

"There are a lot of differences in my relationships with men and women. Coping with the male ego is a real problem to me. I'd like to say I've found men that don't have egos, but I look at the two I sleep with most regularly and they both have outrageous egos that I really have to be careful with. Women are looser. There's not so much on the line. Not the male ego-number going. In relationships between women, sex is just by the way.

"For me, sex with men is a whole different thing from sex with women. The way a man stimulates a woman—for one thing, it's sort of a one-way number. He's the dude. You're the woman. Making love with a woman is different—it's not that I fantasize about being a man when I'm making love to a woman. At that point I'm not fantasizing about what I'm into, which is getting her off. When I'm being the manipulator that's it. That's exactly where I am. You can make a woman do anything. You can build up this charge. Turning on a woman is like an engineering feat. You can just really get into it. It's a power trip and I love it! It's the best power trip you can get into. You're turning somebody on! And you're satisfying them, too. I really enjoy that. When I'm doing that with a woman, I feel a lot more in control.

"I guess in a way it's so with a man, too. But because I like to be the one in control, it's sometimes harder to find a blend with a man. The way a man comes is not nearly as spectacular as with a woman. A woman you can get in ecstasy and keep her in ecstasy. If I had a chance to experience sex with a man as a man does, I think it would be totally different with a male body than it would be a female body. I don't know what it feels like for a man when he's having intercourse, but with a woman I know what's going on. I know all those rushes. With women making love to me, it's just the other side of the coin. It's someone who really knows what she's doing. There's a mirror image going back and forth. It's comfortable. There are some times when I go, 'Wait a minute. I can't remember what to do.' But then again, it's not too often.

"Loving and making love to a man or woman—it's a qualitative difference. Of course, everyone should realize that going down on a man is a whole lot different than going down on a woman. Sometimes oral sex with a man is more of a project. There's not quite so much scenery along the way or fun things to do as there are with a woman.

"I feel equally good about being with both sexes. The only time I don't feel at ease is when I feel sexually threatened. If I'm with a man who's obviously looking at me in terms of fishing bait, 'Ah, look, there's a piece of meat,' then that's one of those times when I'd rather be with a woman. But when some butch is coming on to me, I'd prefer to be with a man."

The women continually used the word "comfortable" when discussing making love with another woman. This is not surprising. Women have been treated as sex objects. Everywhere they turn they see pictures—in magazines, on enormous billboards, dancing across television screens—which project the image of the ideal female. In comparison with these plastic visions, many women believe they are either swathed in fat or scrawny, have pendulous breasts or a concave chest, to say nothing of their cellulite-infested thighs. Radio and TV commercials make them self-conscious about smells emanating from body orifices that were once not even admitted to exist. Many women have a difficult time being at ease with their bodies. But when they are with another woman, these mental concepts of perfection dwindle. They have visual proof that few are close to that Madison Avenue object and tend to feel less concerned about their physical "faults."

As one woman, Melanie, said, "I always feel I have to hold in my stomach when I make love with a man. Am I too hairy? Did I remember to use deodorant? Is that vaginal infection cleared up? I don't have to think about those things if I'm with another woman. We're definitely equals." These moments of insecurity diminish in importance as a relationship lengthens in time, but they are more evident when involved with a man.

Fear of pregnancy was cited by many respondents as another reason they felt more comfortable with a woman. In a woman-to-woman union, this factor is removed. Fran mentioned, "There's a basic fundamental relaxation present. Even though I'm on the pill, when

I'm making love with my husband that nagging doubt is in my head—will or won't I conceive." Strike that concern, and sex for pleasure is much more possible.

The women believed their descriptions of sex and love between women was more detailed and colorful because it *is* a different experience than relations between members of the opposite sex. Sex between men and women is familiar. Sex between women is a new discovery.

Making love to a man is enjoyable because of the uniqueness of the bodies of the two sexes. When sexuality relating to a man, the body parts "fit." Renée is representative in saying that "the concept of two individuals joined together as one is physically and symbolically a beautiful happening. The sensation of a penis inside a woman cannot be duplicated by fingers, tongues, devices, or other paraphernalia. The magic, power, and excitement generated by fellatio is dramatic. Feeling and watching a dormant penis change into a sensitive, sensual organ is pure wonderment. You know when a man is sexually stimulated. A man's orgasm either happens or doesn't. For him there is no way to pretend something that did not occur; thus a woman knows the pattern and rhythm of lovemaking minus any possible deception on his part. Because having intercourse with a man is socially accepted, there are no subconscious thoughts about going against the ordered structure. The affection felt between two humans can be extended from the bed to more public places without being chastised. Man and woman can walk down the street arm-in-arm, embrace, or kiss. These actions are more likely to be greeted with smiles than caustic comments."

Many of the women interviewed are feminists who refuse to hide their sexuality under a blanket of passivity. Furthermore, a number of them no longer feel competition with other women for men's attention. They have discovered a closeness to other women they previously did not believe possible. When dealing with men, their ideal has altered. The men have to be open to change. They, too, have to free themselves from any rigid theories of who must initiate, dictate, and investigate. The women are sexually active. While learning from trial and error what pleases them and what does not, they are trying to stop muffling their feelings.

Another difference frequently mentioned is that the process of lovemaking with another woman is often longer than with a man. There is a slower give-and-take. Many characterize men's approach to sex as working toward an orgasm and women's as looking for an emotional, uplifting experience. Because two women sexually relating to each other often are not as goal oriented as in male/female situations, the pressure to achieve a particular result is absent. Total body contact and appreciation are considered first, instead of primary emphasis being placed on the end product of a single orgasm. And with a woman/woman experience there are often multiple orgasms. In the midst of debates about vaginal versus clitoral, mature versus immature, nymphomaniac versus frigid, women are confronting their own sexual and sensual needs. Many feel that women understand other women's inhibitions, fears, and concerns, but not all men do. Women can identify. Men can only try. When loving a member of the same sex, women do not have to verbalize what actions bring them pleasure. They know what excites them, and they can duplicate it. With a man they have to plow through shyness or embarrassment before being able to communicate what another woman senses intuitively. Concern arises more readily with men over whether they will climax "quickly" enough—before their male partner has finished and lapses into a snooze.

Although many women notice a difference in the quality of the orgasm with a man instead of a woman, finding words to describe it is a challenge. "A vibrational kind of difference." "A different slant or angle of working at something." "Stronger with a man, but not as refined." "Stronger with a woman, because there's been such an incredible build-up." "It's longer lasting, more flowing with a woman." "More profound and deeper with a man." "An orgasm doesn't come solely from vaginal penetration, and that's where many men concentrate. The ears, face, lips, nipples, breasts, stomach, feet, anus, clitoris—anything and everything —should be rubbed, massaged, or kissed, too." "The easiest way for me to come is through oral sex. Some men can't get into that; women can. So I climax more easily and frequently with a woman." "Because a woman doesn't have a penis, she'll be more experimental. She'll use her fingers, tongue, whatever, and play with my vagina, clitoris, and anus all at the same time. With men it's more localized, with just my vagina getting the attention. The orgasm another woman gives me seems to be coming from my whole abdomen. From men it's mainly from the back of my vagina." "An orgasm from a woman is slower, softer, more rolling. With a man the ultimate end is pentration. The rhythm is faster, harder, more pounding." "I don't miss the penis when I'm with a woman, but when I find a man where the fit is right, the climax I get is unbeatable!"

All the women interviewed have had orgasms. While some said they rarely climax the first time they make love with a particular partner, when they learn to know the person better they have no difficulties. Thus all experience orgasms with a high degree of regularity. Only 3 percent stated they have never had a climax while making love with a man, and the same percent had never climaxed with a woman. It is something that takes time. They do not feel this is a static condition but one resulting from lack of experience. It does not lessen their desire to be with that sex.

Between the lines of these generalities about differences in loving men and women are the countless similarities. The comments range from straightforward to mystical. They reveal an enjoyment with a particular type of person, gender aside. As long as there is a bond, a tender understanding between two people, loving and lovemaking is satisfying. The sex of the individuals does not matter. On a purely physical level, by kissing, touching, and stroking any being can sexually stimulate another.

PATRICIA: "There is no difference between being sexually excited by a man or a woman. Put that in capital letters. Once you've gotten through any hang-ups you might have about loving people, either sex can turn you on."

DORIS: "Patience is the key, and any person can have that."

STELLA: "I love kissing, because it can be just like making love. It doesn't matter if it's a man or a woman. I love every part of the body, but I'm not too hot on feet. Give me a shared bubble bath, roaring fireplace with a fur rug in front, green meadows. I'm a romantic who loves love. Let's drink wine, smoke dope and get it on together!"

LIZ: "Men or women . . . they'd better have good legs."

MERLIN: "With both sexes I like to feel they're really horny and want to fuck. At the right moment I find that exciting. Almost like an emotional thing, and they need to do it and are psyched to do it with you. Sexual talk turns me on, a lustful look in the eyes. Beautiful bodies and minds."

JEANNIE: "I like to be touched gently. It doesn't matter if it's a man or woman if they have the capacity to do that."

JACKIE: "I sleep with people who can do it without feeling they own you. Some men and women want to burn their brands on you after making love. When I find a person who wants to love me without jealousy, that's perfect."

CHRISTOPHER: "The quality of touch is the most important factor. Any person who is sensitive and can communicate that physically, emotionally, and spiritually can be satisfying."

AMY: "The capability to love both men and women is a tremendous power. Without that I wouldn't have been able to find solace and unity with the earth mother and the wise old man. Love knows no bounds for me. With each union I discover new areas of myself, new depths to be plumbed. When I love an individual I want a total commitment—no false walls erected, no signs reading 'stop.' We all laugh, cry, sing, worry, eat, sleep, and die. These things hold us together and make us whole. By bringing these thoughts with me to each encounter, I can find no differences. The only difference lies in the soul of each being."

The women touched on their sexual life-styles. They talked about their ages and circumstances the first time they sexually experienced men and women, orgasms, masturbation, open relationships. I never asked for a body count, although some women offered that information. Sally, who is nineteen, has slept with twenty men and five women. Tina is twenty-four and can still remember all the details of the five different men and three women in her life. Annette lost track by the time she was twenty-one. The questionnaire did not ask if they had engaged in group sex, but during the course of our conversations several mentioned this type of experience. Fifteen percent first related to another woman sexually in a ménage à trois. In each instance this was suggested by the male partner.

Rita, a twenty-one-year-old university student, and her husband advertised in the *Los Angeles Free Press* for women to join them for sexual activities. After two such meetings she decided she did not like this method. "It was too cold, too degrading." She followed up by saying, "I think sex has become too commercialized. It's the 'in' thing to fuck as many people—male or female—as a person can. The more you fuck the hipper you are. Intimacy is lost. I've tried sex just for sex's sake, and I felt dissatisfied."

A few other women who are involved in long-term unions with a man said they sporadically try to bring another woman into their relationship. They believe this would be an ideal situation for themselves. While there are these exceptions, the vast majority of their sexual dealings with both sexes is on a one-to-one basis. All engage in cunnilingus and fellatio. A few say they prefer this to penetration, but most view it as simply variety. Only one made any reference to participating in kinky sex such as sado-masochism or bestiality.

Most distinguish between relationships that are exclusive and those that are nonexclusive. Seventeen percent of the interviewees are married and define themselves as having a primary relationship with extramarital affairs. Generally these affairs are with both sexes, but occasionally a woman said that because male/female lovemaking is so readily available within her marriage, most of her outside contacts are with other women. Only in one case did the woman say she might be using her husband as a shield to convey the public image of heterosexuality. All others wanted security, a home and family, but found that temporary outside liaisons add buoyancy and adventure to their lives.

An additional 50 percent of the women are generally involved in nonmonagamous unions. They see monogamy as one more tenet that society tries to foist upon them—a limiting factor because there is much to learn from other people. To them monogamy is an outdated form of behavior imposed on men and women when the "purpose" of two people being together was childbearing and rearing. Subscribing to the principle of exclusive love is too narrow, too restrictive for them. Many rebel against monogamy as a male-imposed concept out of which stems a sense of possession, ownership, and jealousy. Women are not property, they point out. Furthermore, total exclusivity—the pressure to fulfill all the physical, emotional, and spiritual needs of one's partner—is too heavy a burden to place on an individual.

The remaining one-third classify themselves as serially exclusive. Many said they have had enough one-night stands and short-lived affairs to want the ease, comfort, and security of a solid, long-term love. They talked about the difficulty of dividing their energy among several people. It proves confusing and unsatisfying. They feel they cannot work on achieving a meaningful relationship if they have three or four going on at one time. Sometimes the union is with a man, other times with a woman. Yet they still maintain an interest in people of both sexes.

Even in these examples of monogamy, the women try to continue to interact with others on a platonic basis. They feel they should not cut themselves off from friends, activities, and events that are vital to them. Conversely, they should not feign interest in their partners' hobbies or pastimes. They want to remain separate and independent, even when involved in a sexually exclusive relationship. There is also agreement that shifting from being monogamous to nonmonogamous with the same person is exceptionally difficult. Once the ground rules have been established, changing course jeopardizes the union.

There are those who look at sex primarily from the recreational standpoint and those who view it as an extension of love. Some say they do not have to rely on another person for all their sexual enjoyment. Some go long periods of time, up to two years in one woman's case, using only masturbation. To switch that pattern they may go to bars for pick-ups or cruise to meet someone to take home, interspersing one-night stands with relationships of a more lasting nature.

Investigating the subconscious level reveals that bisexual women's dreams and fantasies reflect their overt behavior. Their dreams are populated by men, women, and, occasionally, hermaphrodites. One woman recalled a dream where she was touching a being that had two penises and a vagina. Another described a series of group sex dreams, even though in real life she had never participated in this type of activity. Sometimes in dreams the women changed sex from female to male. This alarmed some of the women but intrigued others. The dreams reported were varied—technicolor, black and white, fragments of events, whole scenarios. In some dreams there was sexual violence, usually perpetrated by men. A few dreamed of themselves as aggressors acting viciously toward other women. Many remembered dreams that had brought them to orgasm. Movie stars—both male and female—appeared in their dreams.

They reported dreaming about both men and women, but dreams of men were more often explicitly sexual while those with women were less specific. Sensual activity—stroking, caressing, bathing—occurs rather than intercourse. Symbolism surfaces in both women-oriented and male-female dreams.

Fantasies present a controlled situation. Many of the women acknowledged that they had not allowed themselves to fantasize about women until they had come to grips with their dual nature. Frightened by what these mental pictures might be telling them, they brushed them aside. Once they overcame their anxieties, women appeared in their fantasies as frequently as men. Some found they thought more about women because women are less accessible than men. Being interested in a man is something they can more readily act upon. Discovering an appealing woman and doing something about it is more difficult. Thus they would fantasize about the "unapproachable, mysterious woman."

The "grass is greener" syndrome often surfaces. When they are involved with men, they fantasize about women. When spending more time with members of the same sex, their daydreams turn to men. Some said they always fantasize when masturbating. Others reported that when making love they think about someone other than their immediate partner.

In this area of questioning it was impossible to obtain percentages because some could not remember any sexual dreams and others never fantasized. To illustrate the variety, I selected six women's responses to this series of questions.

QUESTION: Do you fantasize or dream about sex? If yes, are these fantasies generally related to men, women, or both? Please describe any similarities or differences between your fantasies and dreams about men and those about women.

BRENDA: A profile of Brenda was presented in Chapter 2. Born in 1941, she is single, has a master's degree, and works as a prostitute.

"I used to have very strange dreams when I was very young, before I had any idea what sex was— even prior to fooling around with my cousin in bed. I dream'd I was lashed to a post, stripped down, and some man would come in with a whip. Very heavy-duty dreams. I was always being the passive, brutalized one. All of the good meaningful relationships and dreams I had or even conscious feelings when I was young were directed toward women. And usually I found very similar women. My three best friends at school were all born within one day of each other.

"Now that I'm older I find that it's not that I fantasize more about one sex over the other, but that I fantasize about myself a lot. One thing I've found that's interesting started in my dreams about three years ago. I change sex within myself in a dream. There are times that I've started out a dream as myself and then notice halfway through that I'm still in the dream, but I'm now a man. That puzzled me for a long time. It didn't make much sense. But I've discovered that it's carried over into my conscious life in various relationships. When I'm having a sexual relationship with someone, depending on what my mood is and what my partner's mood is I can make love as though I were a woman or a man. That's regardless of what their sex is. So I can have a relationship with a woman as though I were a woman or as though I were a man. And I can have sex with a man as though I were a woman or a man.

"It doesn't switch off in the same session. The whole session is one way. I've stopped questioning it. I don't care, because I'm comfortable with it. I don't know if it's genes or psychology or what, but I know there are some times that I can be with a man, jump into the sack with him, and suddenly feel as if I'm having a homosexual relationship, even though it's a man. Maybe I'm multisexual, not bisexual. Maybe I have a strange balance of genes. Or perhaps it's all fantasy.

"I guess most of my dreams, starting with those early ones with the whips and chains and leading up to standard rape fear, were based on early childhood experiences. After that I didn't have that many unhealthy dreams. My brother helped a lot. We walked around naked in front of each other all the time, much to my parents' dismay. But, I don't know, there weren't that many conscious fantasies about men. I used to consciously wonder why I wasn't happy with men. Why I felt they were so petty, and you know, everything else involved. I wasn't a man-hater; I just thought men were a little bit inferior. All they cared about was sex, and why in God's name did they only care about that? There was nothing special in it. And then I found out what was so special about sex and I could understand.

"I had a couple of what I consider destructive fantasies with women. Let me clarify that. I didn't fantasize about a woman in the abstract, but when making love to another woman I'd pretend she was a man. I found that destructive and ridiculous. I figured I didn't want to be with that particular woman, if I needed to fantasize about a man in order to get off on her. Then it was that woman I wasn't interested in, and not women in general. I'd had too many success-ful relationships with women to take away from one or two bad experiences. Now I've gotten away from fantasy. It just doesn't occur.

"Before I started really physically relating to women I used to fantasize about them; but again from a psychologically damaging point of view. I'd start to think about a relationship and be sure it would lead to my downfall. I'd have all these terrible visions about being a wanton woman and a man-hater. But once I decided who I was, what I was, what I wanted —they all disappeared. Now they're just nice, healthy fantasies—the few I do have. And they're usually about people I know."

STELLA: Deciding where to begin when describing Stella is difficult. She might be the one you would seek out if you needed guidance in solving a problem. If you were in the doldrums Stella would be ready to go to the movies or take a drive in the country or a walk through the park with you. Hungry? If you called her at mealtime she would immediately invite you over to share her food. Depression set in? Instead of coddling, consoling, or pitying you, she would badger you through humor into a happier frame of mind.

Living the life of a blend of whirling dervish earth mother suits Stella. It has kept her weight under 115 pounds with no exercise required. She almost visibly glows as she plunges from one activity to the next. Her dishwater blond hair is shaped so she doesn't have to bother much with it. Her clothes mirror her spontaneity. She always seems to locate an exotic scarf to wrap around her head or an antique bracelet for her wrist that captures the essence of excitement in her nature.

"I fantasize and dream about sex all the time. When I'm with my lover I'll fantasize even when we're making love. Even when I'm just sitting here I'll daydream a thing with her. Sometimes I'll pretend she's a man. Other times I'll change my name or become a whole different person.

"My fantasies include both scenes and the actual

sex act. My mind will go through this whole thing and
I'll really want to do it, play it out. I watch too many
movies. What can I say? Why should you just have a
general type of sexual thing like going to bed and
making love? I create a story in my head, or maybe
I've seen something on television and it will suggest
something. I'll think, 'Well, far out! I want to get involved in this. I want to do it, see what it's like.' If I'm
someplace, walking down the street or in a restaurant,
I'll look at somebody and this whole fantasy will come
into my head. It's kind of like *Fear of Flying*. You're
actually fucking somebody, because you're thinking it.

"Sometimes I'll fantasize a situation and try and
live it out. That's what I did before I got it on with a
woman. I had known bisexual and gay men, but I'd
never really met a dyke. I had my 'dyke image'—the
truckdriver type, rolled up sleeves and everything. This
woman came into the picture and I knew she was gay.
I thought here she is with all of us girls. When we're
changing clothes she's probably really looking at us.
How would I feel if I were with a whole bunch of men.
That's how I was relating. I thought, 'Oh, she's dis-
gusting, terrible.' The whole thing of liking another
woman was nauseating to me. Then I figured, how
can I do this? How can I say this? Here I'm such
a hypocrite. I tell all these people love who you want
to love, be with who you want to be with, and as soon
as I meet this woman I'm completely against it. Why?

"I did a fantasy trip of relating to her. I planned
the whole thing. I got another friend of mine who was
straight, took my gay friend along, and went to her
house. We took some drugs, and I couldn't wait to
see what would happen. We'd been talking about it—
and then what happened? The gay woman didn't do
anything through the whole thing. It was amazing. She
just shied away from what was going on. I thought she
would be really active, but she wasn't. So that's one
fantasy that never came through.

"I dream about sex too, but sometimes I don't
remember, naturally. I have my prince charming dream.

There he comes. It's like a beautiful thing out in the meadows. I have bizarre dreams if there was a suggestion or I hear something from people. I always fantasize after I hear men talking about how they go to these places, chain the women up, beat and whip them. I'm really frightened to death of the whole thing, but in my dream somebody has got me and I'm all chained up. Really the thought of anyone holding me down with my arms behind me completely freaks me out. I can't stand it. But once in a while I'll dream about somebody finally doing that to me. I'm just screaming and yelling. I always wondered if a woman really would get off on all those sexual things. I don't like anybody to be hitting or beating me."

BARBARA: It is not so much that you notice Barbara's physical appearance. Her face is bare of make-up, her clothes are unobtrusive. But you are aware of her presence. Her voice is quietly melodious, almost forcing you to lean closer to listen. When you speak she gives you her total attention.

Her interests are wide ranging. She plays the harpsichord and the banjo. She's equally adept discussing the business she owns or her feeling on spirituality. The older of two children, she was born in the early 1950s.

"Before I ever went to bed with a woman I remember trying to imagine what it would be like. My fantasies were not general ones, because they really involved one particular woman I was attracted to. I had to imagine in my head what it was like to go to bed with her. Then it seemed natural, but it required fantasizing to get over all the subliminal fears.

"I've had dreams with women, and others with men in them. I had this incredible one about six months ago. I was in a hotel room and David was there. He's a friend who talks about sex all the time. That's all he ever discusses, even though we've never been to bed together. In my dream he wanted to have intercourse. The whole scene had been mapped out for that one reason. After we'd talked about it and there was a whole big sex aura between the two of us, I finally said, 'Maybe we could get together.' Meanwhile in the room across the way, like a New York tenement, I was looking through the windows and there were two women getting it on in bed together. I was watching them in my dream. I was having a ménage à trois in my dream by watching two women while David was making sexual overtures to me.

"Some of my dreams are very symbolic. I can't remember whether they evolved more around men or women, because a lot of times I think you block anything that's unacceptable to you. I can remember consciously thinking, 'Wow, this is a sex dream,' but I wasn't actually involved in intercourse. But I remember getting that feeling about it. I recall one about my boyfriend from high school—we were standing in an ocean of water. I was coming toward him; then nothing more. Also, some of my dreams are completely explicit, the whole sex act from start to finish."

CHRISTOPHER: Christopher is the second of two children. She characterized her mother as spirited, her father as mellow. Tracing the course of her sexual development, she included the facts that she was molested by a family friend when she was ten. She first had intercourse with a man at eighteen, with a woman several months later. Her marriage at twenty lasted for two years. At the time of the interview she was living with her woman lover.

Dance is her primary concern. Five mornings a week she can be found in the rehearsal hall. Weekends she performs in a community dance company. This dedication rules many aspects of her life. It dictates her hair style, a tight bun at the nape of her neck; her clothes, which are leotards and slacks; and her diet, never more than fifteen hundred calories a day.

"When I was very young, three or four, I had a series of dreams concerning being in different bodies. One real strong feeling I had was that I hadn't been in a female body in a long time. I was very unused to this. It was strange. I remember feeling after those dreams, 'What am I here for?' The other people in my family were extremely familiar and there was a great depth of love among us, but still I felt odd being in my female form. In my dreams, fantasies, and real life I was turned on by any tales of Indians, of adventure . . . the traditional male things. I just felt at home with that kind of thinking of myself as a male.

"Also at an early age, and continuing for a long period of time, I remember specific dreams where I'd be right in the middle of something and couldn't complete it. I'd be in the midst of making love, usually with a woman, but I was in a male body. And there was this real heart-rending feeling that I couldn't complete it. I couldn't love a person or have them love me. This led to a lot of confusion for awhile.

"When I started getting into relationships with guys when I was in my late teens, I'd dream about women. Then, after becoming involved with women, I'd find myself dreaming about men. It was really crazy. Maybe it was compensation in whatever images. Now that I'm older, more at peace with myself, I think our sexuality has a lot to do with where the soul is on an experiential level. Wherever we are, if we need to work out some experiences of seeing things from another viewpoint, then we will by our own will one way or another get another body that will teach us that. That's why those dreams no longer concern me."

NANCY: A business major, Nancy attended Stanford for undergraduate work, California-Berkeley for her master's degree. She is content being single but sometimes thinks she may have a child. Her future plans range from remaining in the business world to getting into the production end of theater or going to law school.

"I dream and fantasize about both men and women. Sometimes right in the middle of the dream the men will turn into women. I don't recall the opposite ever taking place, women changing into men. I like that.

It's interesting. For awhile I had a lot of snake dreams, which I felt were very symbolic or indicative of my emotions at the time. One in particular was very vivid. A male friend and I were walking through a field when suddenly we both saw a snake moving through the underbrush. Right at the moment I asked him for help, he ran off. And I got bitten. I started trying to escape. The next thing I realized was some woman had appeared and helped me. That's how the dream ended.

"Sometimes in my dreams I can't tell whether I'm a man or a woman. I'm making love to someone, and I realize it's a woman. I'm sort of like a man, but I'm me. Other times it's as if I were making love to myself, because I realize I'm both people. It's really neat with all those changes going on."

ANNETTE: Annette was born in 1949. Her father died when she was three, and her mother remarried. Her half-brother was born when Annette was eight. She felt strong affection towards her parents. Although she was raised with warmth and love, sexuality played little part in her upbringing. At what her mother considered the right time, she gave Annette *Ann Landers Talks to Teen-agers About Sex*. She recalled, "It didn't tell me anything except I shouldn't do anything." She describes her life as "full and rich." For the last year she has been living with a man while continuing to relate to women.

"Fantasies and dreams have played a part in my life for a long time. When I was about thirteen I had a girl friend whom I used to get together with. We both liked girls and boys a lot at that age. We'd spend the night at each other's house and pretend that one of us was a male. We'd talk about boys and masturbate. She'd had more actual experience. I'd only kissed a little. We'd take turns feeling each other's tits, what there was of them, and making up all kinds of fantasies. They'd usually revolve around things we were into. As we got interested in the Beatles, we'd be with one of them. At that time I think I was pretty much tuned to the male psyche. I'd be thinking she was the male.

"What's strange is that even though it felt good, I recall feeling a certain amount of guilt. The guilt didn't stem from the fact that we were both little girls but the impure thoughts I had. The Catholic church didn't tell you it was wrong to like your girl friends. What was bad was the fact I was thinking about being with men.

"Now my life and ideas have changed. I feel I have a pretty full life right now because I'm living with one person. That changes my entire attitude, and my energies go more toward him and my time with him. So my sexual fantasies have to do with just us doing things together. Sometimes I do think about other people, being with them. Those fantasies I feel I live out in different situations. I fantasize about things I'd like to do.

"I've had some weird dreams the last few days. They're the most prominent, because they're so recent. The one I had a couple of days ago really freaked me out. My grandmother was in it, only it wasn't really her but a grandmother figure. In the dream she'd been raped by four or five guys. I sort of rescued her from them. After they went away, she was distraught. Then I went up to her and grabbed her tits. When I woke up I went, 'Whoa! This is really heavy.' In the long run I really helped her, made her feel better, but it was that little instantaneous sleaze that I did that bothered me.

"I watch 'Star Trek' almost every night, and I had a funny dream about Mr. Spock. I remember that all of a sudden there he was with a huge hard-on. It was disproportionately large, and because of the perspective of the dream it looked as if it came out of him from another plane. His whole cock with this enormous hard-on was bright blue. I thought, 'Wow, what a neat cock!' I was looking at it and touching it. Then I remembered he was kissing me, and on the end of his tongue he had this tiny ball. He'd move his tongue back and forth rapidly, like a frog might do. It freaked me out and I woke up after that.

"It's only recently that I've been having really sexual dreams. Usually my dreams have a lot of people in them whom I haven't seen for awhile. I don't think other than that incident with my grandmother that I have ever dreamt about being with a woman or women in a sexual manner. Once in awhile I have a dream that involves actual sex, but very rarely. If I do, I don't remember them. Most of them are just short incidents where something weird happens. It doesn't seem like I ever have complete sequences in my dreams."

5.

Companions
and Confidants

Bisexual women do not spend the majority of their time cavorting from one sexual encounter to the next. Although they are often creative and innovative, when it comes to variety in sexual expression they have not cornered the market. Beds are not the only place where people relate sexually. Anyone—heterosexual, homosexual, or bisexual—who has an active sex life can recount experiences indoors and out. The floor, tables, chairs, bathtubs, gardens, beaches, woods, meadows—are all possible places for making love. Some explore all these options, while others restrict their activities to the bedroom.

Sex is as important to bisexuals as to anyone else, but not all-consuming. Concern with the mundane work of daily existence is universal, and bisexual women are no exception to the rule. Eating food on a regular basis and keeping a roof over their heads are on the list of priorities. They, too, must sleep, wash, and make routine trips to the store, laundromat, doctor, bank, and post office. Someone must clean house, scrub bathrooms, prepare meals, wash dishes, and iron. And because most of these women are single, they are usually that someone. Bills must be paid. Most are employed, responsible for themselves without supplements from family, friends, or the government. Even those who are married often hold jobs outside the home. They have good days and bummers.

They have friends they love dearly but never sleep with. With other friends, they carry feelings to a physical plane. They have sex because they feel a strong physical attraction, are bored, lonely, feel tension, or want a little fun. They have relationships of various durations and intensity. No two emotional time clocks function at the same speed. Rarely do two people start and stop caring in the same way at the same moment. At one time or another all have brought the sexual aspect of a relationship to an end. All have experienced rejection themselves. Having explored their sexual lifestyles, let's look at other facets of their characters. What happens when a sexual relationship cools? Can the relationship be reestablished on a platonic level?

A composite of responses reveals a variety of adjustments. One point should be remembered. In the beginning 72 percent of their relationships with women and 32 percent with men developed from friendships. Add or substract sex, and the original foundation is still there. When the union is first based on mental exploration and then moves on to include sex, the ties run deep. The women find it rewarding to keep the lines of communication open after the sexual fires have cooled. Sex becomes one more area in which to know a person, but not the most vital. As Brenda said, "Sex between two people is not all that important. It's just like anything else. I shoot pool, and if I shoot a good game one night, fine. If I shoot a rotten game, I just shrug my shoulders, because I know that some night after that I'll shoot another good game. I treat sex the same way. If it's a good part of a relationship, fine. If it's not, it doesn't really matter. My ego isn't hurt by it. Sex, like everything else, is a matter of taste, timing, and a meeting of the minds."

Where a sexual relationship grew out of a friendship, it is deeply distressing to have the person withdraw both as a companion and lover. Some speak of trying to "create partners for life" or a "family of friends."

Different people answer different needs. For some sex is a primary need; for others emotional needs are more pressing. Everyone evolves and changes. If two people are moving in the same direction, the situation is ideal. If they are not, the relationship must alter.

When sex between friends is over, the formula for reestablishing communication on another level is simple yet difficult to employ—for both the one who feels rejected and the one who has withdrawn. Usually the instigator must clearly state: "I want to be your friend. I do not want to sleep with you, but I am still concerned about you as another human being. Our ways have diverged. We are distant. But the basic issues that dissipated our sexual compatability have not destroyed all other feelings."

A little less than 40 percent of the women said they were able to move from a sexual to a nonsexual level with both men and women. An additional 35 percent said this was easy with women, frustrating or impossible with men. Fifteen percent reported finding it very difficult or impossible to do it with either sex. They are jealous people. The sexual aspect is intrinsic. When that is gone, the relationship is finished. They feel insecure, unwilling either to make the first move or to respond when friendship is tendered. Others explained that they go through individuals as chapters in a book. Once the chapter is completed, they move on. They live in the present, find excitement in new people rather than in memories or shared experiences from long-lived relationships. The remaining 10 percent saw the process as an individual matter unrelated to gender. They wanted to maintain contact with some people and not with others.

In analyzing why there is a difference between changing a relationship with a man versus a woman, they presented several theories. Sex-role stereotypes play a major part. With men there is often the built-in expectation they are going to be lovers first, then friends. That is hard to amend. When a man is accustomed to acting on sexual energy in a relationship with a woman, often too little remains when that element is withdrawn. There is then no basis for companionship or emotional support.

Many women felt that situations have to be worked through more cautiously with men. Their egos must be handled gingerly. They think men tend to feel personally rejected, not understanding relationships as complex, multitiered experiences. Because traditional sex roles are more firmly adhered to when there is male/female interaction, confusion and tension are created when that pattern is broken. After this type of sexual union is finished there is often concern over who makes the first call—what kind of overture. A number of women reported that being assertive, aggressive, and confident makes the man ill at ease and weakens his self-image.

When a woman-to-woman love ends, the dynamics are different. Women are more used to relating to each other on only a platonic level. While mutual attraction between a male and female is more often acted upon, our culture gives women less leeway in dealing with a member of the same sex. As Tina said, "With another woman if you care enough to go against society and sleep with her, there have to be a lot of common interests and powerful emotions. So when you aren't sexually interested anymore, you still have something to go on in maintaining a friendship."

Elaine offered an opinion on why there is a difference in relating to men and women when sex is no longer present. "Somehow I have the feeling of less responsibility when I'm with a woman. I guess that's because we're both female. We can operate as we go along instead of having these imprinted pictures of 'that's what a woman does and this is what a man does.' There's more freedom between women. When the sex is over we have no hard and fast rules to follow. We can wing it in how we function. Who does what first."

Many of the respondents characterized sex as an integral part of a male/female relationship but just one facet of a woman-to-woman affair. Eliminate it from a union, and more of a bond remains with another woman than with a man.

The majority believed you create your own environment. They would not set up situations that were intimidating or made them feel uncomfortable. If they still loved a person and would be hurt by seeing him or her minus the sexual aspect, they would shy away from them until they could handle their feelings. The reverse is true also. If they knew they had hurt another person but wanted to maintain the relationship on another level, they would avoid pressuring that individual into accepting the situation on their terms.

When having sex rather than making love is the basis of interaction, intellectual and emotional attachment is minimal, although some women classified this type of sexual involvement as a shortcut to learning more about a person. "Sex with somebody can make you realize quickly where they're coming from," Liv said. "Selfishness in bed often corresponds to the rest of their personality. Timidity, aggression, role-playing —all these can be discovered in one brief romp. Then I know—move out of my life. I don't have time for you. Of course the opposite happens, too. Beautiful, wonderful characteristics can come out. 'Hey, this person wants me to find pleasure. This person is warm and giving sexually. He or she might be worth knowing more about.' It's like a crash course in who they are."

Bisexual women do not sleep with every person they meet. They are as selective and discriminating as any other random group of women. Their lives encompass many people they relate to solely on a platonic basis. When seeking companionship or emotional support, 50 percent replied they initially turn to other women, 10 percent to men, and 40 percent said it depends entirely on the activity, problem or individual.

Often those who answered "women" left it at that. They offered no qualifiers, no distinctions. A few responded by saying they prefer women's company for "political and personal reasons." Others cited more profound bonds, a greater empathy because they are the same sex. Cindy capsulized this response: "My personal opinion, which I share with numerous people, is that women will always be closer than a man and a woman simply by virtue of being the same sex. Even though I have lots of male friends who are wonderful and I'm very close with, there are deeper, more emotional links with women as far as friendships go. They last longer. The energy is heavier. But there's a balance. I think I must have the same amount of male friends as women."

Patricia explained the emotional unity she feels with other women in this way. "I get more understanding from women because we're on the same wavelength. The emotional make-up of men and women is different, and I've felt that difference. It's easier for one woman to identify with the cycles, the ups and downs another female can go through in one day. But it's not like I haven't had men attempt to understand my emotional make-up and try to gratify it. It's just harder for them. With a man you have to intellectualize—verbalize—your feelings. He has to comprehend where you're coming from in his head. With a woman you don't have to explain as much. That's why I go mainly to women for companionship and support."

For those who are now feminists there was not an exact moment or situation that brought about this decision, but rather a combination or culmination of circumstances. Enrollment in women's studies courses sometimes speeded this change. Occasionally the interviewees talked about participating in demonstrations for women's issues. Many had signed petitions for discontinuing the dispensing of DES, the passage of the Equal Rights Amendment, equal access to crafts unions, and employment in police and fire departments. The title of the first feminist literature they read and identified with is no longer important. What matters is that they are continuing to read, learn, and grow. The precise time when they said, "We are not 'girls,' but women" is not the point; the word choice is not a semantic hang-up but stems from their evolving self-concept.

While they are reevaluating themselves and rebelling against the stereotypical male/female roles, finding men who are moving in a similar direction is difficult. Grace was representative in that she acknowledged the desire to have men in her life yet felt frustrated in dealing with them once they were there. Too often the men were either slow to tune into her beliefs or took her altered commitments lightly.

"Lately I'm having trouble relating to men," she explained. "Mentally, OK, but when it comes to emotional contact women provide me with much more empathy. The ideas presented in the women's studies courses I've been taking are changing my head and the concepts I had. They've also made me very touchy. It's as if I've awakened to certain beliefs that are important to me but not to most men. I find that many things they say and do are just extremely stupid. I'll try to reason with them very logically, give them arguments why they shouldn't say that or why they shouldn't feel that way; why they're not investigating another way of looking at situations. However I've tried to affect a change, I've found that often men are incredibly irritating. They'll put down my feelings without even really listening to me. They become very paternalistic and superior and just nod. It's absurd the way they do that. I've found that to be a pattern in so many men I know.

"Finding the patience to communicate with men is hard, because what's really of sustaining interest to me is exploring my own consciousness and that of women in general. I've been reading books on the image of women in film—how that has been portrayed and how it's degenerated in inverse proportion to women's emergence in the working world. This is something that's very close to me. I'm trying to make some changes in my life so I can be more economically important to myself and the world. I've found that men have little understanding, little tolerance for that as a female desire.

"They revert to statements like 'Well, women are getting favoritism right now.' I heard one man say, 'Any book a woman wrote would be published very easily, but it'd be trash. Women have never made any good films. Women have never produced any art of merit.' Real bullshit. I've found dealing with that is very draining on my energy."

Grace and others were influenced by their knowledge of such fields as mysticism, reincarnation, and Eastern philosophies. Several mentioned that each person not only has male and female parts but in past lives has been both sexes. Grace continued, "I'm very involved in mystical studies. I believe that men need women and women need men to further their development—both sexual and spiritual—and to expand their understanding of who they truly are and the complexities of their nature. For men to put down and confine women, not examine the woman in themselves and allow this woman to develop, is limiting on their part. I'm meeting women right now who, I'm happy to say, are very complex people. I love the nurturing aspects, the warmth in my relationship with other women. I just prefer the way women relate to the world. It's very comforting and comfortable."

Judith hesitated before answering the emotional support question. "It's tough to draw a strict line between men and women for this question. I notice that lately I'm enjoying the company of women more than men. But there's something about male energy—the kind that's stimulating to me and necessary—that I miss when there aren't men in my life. There is something in men that makes me really like to have a couple of good ones around. But are they ever hard to find! Many aren't as together as the women I know.

"I first started joining women's groups in about 1967. I became very involved with the beginnings of feminism in college. I felt there was a difference in the way I looked at women then from the way I had before when they were just my 'girl friends.' For the first time I met women who were interested in something other than clothes and getting married. It was a real eye-opener.

"I know it's hard for men to understand the changes women are going through. If both sexes could be presented with a blank tablet, with no rules, and start from scratch it might be easier. But we don't have that. Men have to learn we have moved beyond simplistic issues to real gut level problems. How much of our lives do we compromise for another individual? How much of ourselves do we give up to make a man happy? And we're saying—'Wait a minute. I'm a person too. I'm not going to be some man's left foot, his silent appendage. Decisions should be mutually arrived at. Both brains should be tapped.'

"It's so much easier not to change. There are still women out there who don't give a damn about feminism—who want to be taken care of. Why should men bother with those of us who demand to think for ourselves? But then they see the pressure would be removed from them if universal feminism were the order of things. They'd have the freedom to be more human, more rounded. We have so much to learn from each other. I'm not going to give up. I'm spending more time with women, but I can't and won't turn my back on the other half of the population. I just wish men would stop fighting these changing roles so much."

Ramona felt that her changing impression of the sexes has come from gaining more experience with people, instead of directly from the impact of the women's movement. "Generally it's been easier for me to relate to women. And I've had more successful friendships with them than men. About 80 percent of the companionships I've had with men have been as lovers. At the same time I've had that, I've also had very close dealings with women all along.

"Now that I'm getting older it's becoming easier for me to relate to men as people and not as sex objects.

I can look at a man, be with him, enjoy him as a person, and not necessarily want to go to bed with him."

Although Merlin spends more time with men, the women's movement has touched her life as well. She was trying to integrate her friendships more and understand the motives behind her actions. "If I want to do something or have a problem to solve, I tend to seek out the company of men. I've gone through a lot of thinking about this because I consider myself a feminist, yet I have to confront the fact that in certain ways I feel much more at ease with men. For instance at a party I feel men are more accepting of me, and that kind of disturbs me. Most of my friends are men.

"I think it has to do with competition between women. I really try to work that out, but it's rough. When I was growing up my parents weren't very social, and I was very shy. Much of that time there weren't many people around, so it was often me against my mother. We had some terrible fights, especially when I was a teen-ager. My brother was a companion, and my father was very supportive. He had faith in me and still does—more than my mother.

"Feminism has helped me. It's created problems also, but I'd rather have the problems than be the way I was. I don't think I had an orgasm until I was twenty, even though I'd been fucking pretty steadily since I was sixteen. It was not right for women to respond sexually, because that meant you were a slut. It was most important that the man got off. I mean I didn't even know what an orgasm was. I didn't need to have one, but he did. That caused problems, because I went out with one boyfriend for three years who always wanted to fuck. I had it in my mind I had to do that or he wouldn't like me. About 90 percent of the time I didn't enjoy it, but I did it because I felt he was going to reject me. When I started feeling different, resentment came out. I thought, 'Goddamn it, I've been left out all these years. Just a doormat for somebody else's sexuality.'

"Feminism opened me up to feeling closer to women

as sisters. I broke up with that guy, and the women's movement was just beginning to happen. I started reading everything I could get my hands on. I'd think, 'I've felt that way for so long and I'm not putting up with that shit any more.' It made me see that all this time I had totally devalued my female friends. If a guy asked me to go somewhere and I'd already made plans with another woman, I'd just say, 'Sorry, Sally, I'm going out with Johnny.' She'd understand, even if she got a little pissed off. I realized I'd gone through five guys, but these women had been my friends for years—why am I saying they're not as important as some man? So I'm working, I'm trying, and I hope to grow in my feelings toward both sexes."

Many of the women expressed the belief that a perfect world would be one in which human interchange is based on personality and immediate need rather than sex. They felt that men and women must become integrated beings—uni- or pansexual. Character traits once attributed only to one sex should be encouraged in both. Knowledge of individuals, people, and society increases through contact, not through isolation from a portion of the population. They were convinced that an eclectic synthesis of the best of both sexes is worth striving for, and believed, "The woman who most needs liberating is the woman in every man, and the man who most needs liberating is the man in every woman."

Several women discussed their attitudes toward that point of view. Stella was spending more time with women, but she felt a void in her life. "I'm starving for male drive and aggressiveness. Why shouldn't women try to develop some of that, too? Why shouldn't men learn that there are moments when they can let up and be a little more human instead of always trying to be supermen? I like strong, on-the-go people, who are never too tired. If there's something to be done, do it, and then move on to do what you really enjoy.

"Don't diddle around. Sometimes I think women are great at that. We have to get out of falling back on those built-in excuses. 'It's my period. I've got cramps. I can't get out of bed today. Whine!' Maybe men feel lousy, but they hide it better. Take a little maleness from men, soften it up with warmth, mothering from women, and we'd come up with a good person."

Elaine praised and blamed both men and women. "As friends I probably spend more time with women, but I find it very frustrating to get anything done with them. Then I like men better. Need a partner for a business? At this point I'd have to go to a man. Men seem to be a lot more responsible, punctual, and drive-oriented. Certainly they're more organized. Have you ever sat through a women's meeting thinking, 'My God, when are we ever going to get anything completed.' Collectives are fine, but they slow things down so much.

"I do feel sorry for many men. So often they're oppressed by all the stereotypes. We've all put women in cages and kept ourselves submissive by doing this. But as a result men are in a much tighter cage because women are now working their way out. We can have equal jobs, equal opportunity. We can leave men. But men are generally stranded because they're stuck in this whole process. It's not easy for a man to switch course. They're having to go through just as much of a learning process to reorient themselves to treating women as people, not objects or property. Women have to do some of that, too. We can't demand things without coming up with the strength of character to deal with our gains once we have them.

"It would be perfect if I could just tap the person closest to me for whatever my wants or projects might be. If we can ever find the keeper of the keys to those cages we've erected around ourselves we'd be so much better off."

While seeing differences between the sexes, Gretchen was trying to lessen those in herself and those closest to her. "Before this summer I would have automatically answered 'women' to that question," she began. "Women are much better friends. They understand, console, comfort. They're able to talk about feelings.

I usually end up with lots of women friends. Then I've gone through periods, changes, where I was the tomboy type and hung around with men all the time. Women seemed kind of weak and wishy-washy to me. After I became a feminist, kind of, I had all women friends. Now just lately I've been thinking I can't ignore men, because they offer me something too.

"On the companionship level I view them in different ways. I get something from men that so far I haven't been able to find in women. It seems to be intellectual, rational, more than anything else. It's some kind of a challenge or an image to measure up to. They think and see things in another perspective. Looking at things from their viewpoint is valuable to me.

"Men and women fill two different sets of needs for me. I can be satisfied by either one on his or her own. With my relationship with my male lover, who's bisexual, we're trying to develop it to where he's able to give me more and more of the feminine things. And I'm able to offer him more of the masculine qualities. There has got to be a balance somewhere. I'm glad we're trying to do that, but still I feel a need for women."

Liz spoke for many of the respondents in saying, "I try to look beyond the sex of the individual, get back to what kind of a person he or she is. I'd rather spend more time with interesting people, no matter what sex they are, than with bores."

Are their relating patterns constant, or do bisexual women assume different roles when interacting with men than with women? Approximately 60 percent sensed they behaved differently toward men, and being aware of this fact, were attempting to change their actions. Many credited the women's movement for guiding them through this transition. A problem cannot be resolved without first acknowledging its existence. By incorporating feminist concepts—economic, philosophic, political, and social equality between the sexes —into their lives, they have increased awareness of sexist behavior and support in overcoming it. They no longer felt isolated. They realized they are products of their environment and conditioning, but that they do not have to act or react in those expected ways.

They felt that change inevitably follows discovery of the cause of this role-playing. They talked about not wanting to slip on a female mask when it serves a purpose—not pretending to be unintelligent to gain something from a man; not expecting to reap the rewards of feminism when still demanding that men provide total economic support and accept all decision-making responsibilities. They were convinced that honest relationships result from clearly stated feelings, that no woman should be afraid to be herself when in the company of men. To be one's true self only with women, they point out, is not being fair to oneself, or men.

Many of the women admitted that they did fall back into stereotyped roles. And it disturbed them when they did not measure up to their own expectations. Some felt that the ability to overcome role-playing is a result of growing older and having experience with more people in varying situations. Through experience and experimentation they have learned not to turn solely to men for sexual gratification and love, and to women for emotional support and companionship. Both offer both.

Many bisexual women believed that if they were threatening to another individual, that was his or her problem—not theirs. They realized some people would not allow them to be completely open with them. The respondents felt these people were not worth the effort of trying to present a realistic picture of themselves.

Many of the women saw their evolution from stereotypical female to independent women as a series of stages. The initial step was discerning whether they adopted different behavior with women and with men—and some had difficulty deciding. They wished they could videotape their behavior with an instant replay for careful analysis. Among those who felt a distinct dichotomy, some went into a period of withdrawal. By turning primarily inward and to other women, they felt they could clear their lives of role-playing clutter, and after this self-imposed evaluation period be ready for "reentry" into the mainstream of life. A number of women who had been through this process said they were often hard-pressed to find men who had moved in the same direction.

Avoiding role-playing in the business and academic worlds seemed to be a particular problem for many. The best intentions can dissipate when a threat to economic security enters the scene.

Jackie saw herself as still in the process of learning how to relate to both sexes in an equal manner. Frustrated by dividing her personality in parts, she is currently spending more time with women. "I'm not the same person when I'm around men as I am when I'm with women," she said. "That's one reason I've been concentrating my energy on women. It was actually when I got into feminism that I made the decision I was really not interested in relating to men any more in the assigned roles. Feminism gave me the social context to recognize I was different. When I was with a man, even though I didn't want to or he didn't want me to, often these traditional roles came into play. I'd find myself doing things and questioning how I was behaving. It wasn't worth it to me. I never felt free to assert the kind of influence that I feel free doing with my women friends. I'm a planner. Also I like to control my activities, and women can do that by manipulation of men, but they can't do it straight. And I like to do it straight. I haven't been able to do that with men.

"I don't think I would have come to this point without the growing force in my life of the women's movement. The movement helped me say, 'This is what's happening and this is what I'm doing.' In my sexual life nothing different has happened. I continue to see both sexes, but with men there's not much more than getting it on. Feminism gave me a sense of strength and support so I could act on my feelings. One reason I moved to California was because in Ohio I felt very alone. I knew the women's movement and acceptance of varying forms of sexuality were more possible here. I came to the Bay Area because I knew per capita there were more gay and bi people here than any place else. I thought, 'That's part of my life, and I might as well be where I can pursue that.'

"I've noticed changes in myself. I'm feeling better about the person I am. Now I feel like expanding my emotions and seeing if there are any men around with whom I can relate honestly on all levels. I hope there're a few who are changing in the way I've been."

Liz believed she was basically the same person when dealing with men and women until it came to her business. As a free-lance film-maker, her main contacts are with men. That is when the trouble begins. "Roles are much ingrained in both sexes. It's subtle, and the switch is subtle. But nonetheless I think it's there. There're certain expectations that men have which you kind of fall into unless you're pretty canny about it. I've become aware of that over the years and rarely do it with friends. Unfortunately there are situations which call the mechanisms into play. I think this is one of the reasons the work I'm doing now is bad for me. It makes me vulnerable to male clients, because they know I've got to have access to their budget before I can make the film I want to make. Or it means that I haven't really convinced them that they have to make it. Another variable might be I've convinced them, but they'll hold back on the budget unless I sleep with them. So that's a contract down the drain as far as I'm concerned. I don't take bribes either, and I've been offered a few of those. In that situation my role changes. It has to. Being a woman in that situation becomes very complex.

"You can play this game a little bit just on the human level, the flirtation thing because it's kind of fun. On the other hand, if you once get past that point, whatever it is in the game, then you not only change roles, becoming more female than person or more female than professional—I've also lost the contract because I won't complete the game. This happens with men. It doesn't happen or hasn't happened in my experience with women. I want to always be true to myself, but it's frustrating. I've got to eat, and sometimes that necessity gets in the way."

The battle to overcome role-playing was continuing for Judith. She was trying to react in a similar manner with both sexes, but her progress had reached a plateau. Now it is moving forward. "Because I'm threatening to a lot of men," Judith said, "I've developed this strange conditioning where I know I shut off a part of myself that's very basic to me. This happens mainly when I'm with a man I might want to have a relationship with or feel that there's something happening emotionally. For the last couple of months I've really been working on this. I've come a long way, so that now I'm more honest all the way around.

"Many of my feelings result from being involved in the heavy academic atmosphere at Harvard. The English department is very negative toward any women who are accepted in the graduate program, because the professors are against having any dealings with Radcliffe. I had to sublimate much of what was going on inside me as a woman for my academic self. When I was with women I thought I could really be my whole self. I started doing that once I took a break from school. Then, when I met men who were that kind of person—still into the roles—I would immediately turn into that other person. Finally I called a halt. I am going to be a total individual. I will not be a charade or caricature to please people."

"Sometimes I go through a personality change when I'm with men," Nancy reported. "I can easily get into this kind of good little girl pattern. Ol' Goodie Two-Shoes comes along in her little pinafore trying to do everything nice. Then I revert back to my natural bitchy self. I was individualistic as a child and still am as an adult. But I think I'm more even in relating to people now. I just don't take that stuff men dish out where I have to be sweet, silent, and skip along to their tune.

I'll tell them what I think. Consequently, a lot of men have told me, as they were running away, that I really scared them. So I've spent a lot of time minus the company of men. Women roll with my character more. They don't scare as easily.

"What I look like on the outside is important to me, too. I'm into an attractiveness bag. Why should I let myself look like a shrew when I'm with women and get flashy when men walk in? I'm still a little caught up in that, because I sense men consider outward appearance more important than other women do. But it's not that much to me. Maybe it's a power or ego thing. I don't like people telling me I'm ugly or not attractive. I just don't want to deal with it. I want to move around clearly, and I find that it makes it a lot easier to do that when I look good.

"When I'm in my house I just do whatever I want to do. If someone comes to visit me, some men and most women, I just wear what I happen to be wearing, look the way I happen to look. There's something about going outside into the world—it's like a vulnerable position, leaving my house.

"I've been a feminist for a long time, and sometimes it's depressing to walk into a room full of feminists. I'm into trying to look as good as I can. I like to look sexy sometimes for men and women, but at the same time I feel guilty because I sense I have to explain why I want to do this. I think it's natural for people to want to be attractive.

"It's obvious from the female kind of men around that they'd use make-up to enhance their looks if it were more universally permitted. The ones who don't care about it being permissible do it now. I'm narcissistic enough to want to adorn my body the way it pleases me at the moment. I really dislike women looking like men. It turns me off. The heavy duty women who cut their hair and wear overalls seem so crazy to me. I don't see the point of it. I understand the psychological reasons, but it seems to me an accolade to men's power to try to be like them. Those women are just removing the softness, the good in women.

"We're a blend of the inside and out. If we're ever going to be free of roles we have to work on both. I'm just as strong and independent a woman with my hair looking halfway decent and my clothes together as when I'm in jeans and a T-shirt. I don't judge people's worth by what they have on, but why do so many feel they have to make a political statement with every article of clothing. Let's tone it down a little."

Bisexual women are not unique when it comes to adopting differing roles with men and women. Most are aware, to some extent, of role-playing but, they, like the majority of women, have not completely overcome those patterns as yet.

How the respondents view themselves in comparison with the average American female is difficult to discern. Are they more or less aggressive, independent, goal-oriented, introspective, inhibited, fulfilled? The question is relative. Compared with her circle of friends, a woman might be considered retiring, while measured against a hypothetical average she might seem a model of assertiveness. Are most women truly passive, nurturing, home-centered? If the norm is goal-oriented, what might those goals be? To bake a perfect pie? To have the largest home on the block? To make it through the day without screaming at the kids? Or do women have more spiritual goals—to become a better person; to love another individual fully and well? Does introspection translate to constant worrying about oneself? Does it indicate a person who is concerned solely with his or her individual programs? A blanket statement about inhibition is equally difficult. Even the most confident person has experienced queasy moments when confronted by alien situations. People can be inhibited if threatened but tremendously outgoing in familiar surroundings. Fulfilled? Often the answer depends on the day the question is asked.

Keeping all these variables in mind, this purely subjective question was posed to the women interviewed.

What is your self-image in comparison with the average woman? A little more than 15 percent declined to answer. They felt women have traditionally been oppressed by stereotypes and expressed their disapproval of categorizing by not responding to the question. Approximately 85 percent characterized themselves as more aggressive than the average woman. Some preferred the word "assertive," feeling the connotations are more attuned to their personalities. Most viewed themselves as leaders more than followers. They were strong and confident, challenging their environment.

Eighty-five percent felt they were independent. Their value judgments were based on fact and emotion. Responsibility for their own financial and emotional security makes independence a reality in their lives, whether or not they are married or living with another individual. They make countless decisions, function efficiently on their own, and do not continually spin toward their partners for help.

There is an even split on the question of goal-orientation. Fifty percent considered themselves more goal-oriented than the average, the other half less so. This division comes from society's definition of a goal, equating it with professional and material success. Those who defined themselves as less goal-oriented felt they were not searching for the prestigious job title, large paycheck, or abundance of material possessions. They lived for the day and found happiness in more nebulous objectives. Thus the responses to this question ran the gamut from immediate to life goals.

Where Liv's hopes centered on supporting herself by her art and creating a living environment conducive to her personal needs, Doris concentrated on the present. She wanted to have a pleasant evening. Amy would have liked to buy land and move to the country. Helen answered, "I'm not ambitious, if that's what you mean. I don't have any goals like going after a master's degree. I'm goalless in that sense, except to keep decently ahead of the tax collector and have enough to eat and wear."

Some goals are more abstract—"to be comfortable with myself," "to communicate as much love as I can through whatever medium." Others had specific ideas that reflect the traditional concept of a proper goal. They wanted to be professional musicians, artists, dancers, lawyers, doctors, or therapists. Often the women mentioned both concrete plans and emotion-linked ideals. Renée would be pleased with professional success as an actress, but also described her life goals as "to be happy, to love as many people as I can. But not love them because I want love in return. I want to be able to let go, relax, and let things come to me."

Michele's goals were varied, ranging from wanting to help build a feminist socialist revolution to training to be a primal therapist. Judith was torn between wanting to travel and making a home base for herself in order to write the great American novel. A few of the women felt they should be more goal-oriented, but were happy the way they were. Some mentioned parental pressure to "do something" with their lives. Cindy said she always prided herself "on being horribly nongoal-oriented," then added that her mother was continually asking her what she was going to do when and if she grew up. "My mother thinks I'd be more content if I had some 'direction,' but there's not really one thing I want to do. My main concern is to go through as many parts of my capabilities and talents as I can, rather than channel myself into one career. There're lots of things I want to do. I want to travel, write, work with people, go into politics, do community things, have fun. I could go on and on. There may be things I don't even know about that I'll discover I want to do."

"This year?" was Maria's response. "My picture of nirvana is walking through the woods, going home at night to a house with a warm bed, gas stove, hot and cold running water, and a shower. Toss in a career as a commercial artist or calligrapher, and there I am."

Grace was undecided. She wanted to be a professional, but she was not certain in which field. Right now it was between directing in theater and being an attorney. But her main emphasis was on money. "That's important to me," she said. "To have money, to be comfortable, I've been struggling for a long time, having to compromise a lot."

For Gretchen, material goals were minimal. The ones she listed were to know herself more, develop her potential, be able to express herself better. She laughed as she said, "I don't have any goals like to get married and have children or go to medical school and save the world."

Brenda was in agreement with her, adding, "I stopped setting goals several years ago. I've seen too many people who have a dream and decide, 'This is what I want to do by the time I'm fifty. This is how much money I want to make.' They spend their whole lives working toward that goal and get there, and they've lost sight of it by the time they've gotten there. They don't really want what they've worked for. So I just take one day at a time."

Viewing goal-orientation from the perspective of her thirties, Fran answered, "I used to have life goals a long time ago, but that's changed considerably. When I think of life goals I usually think of my career goals. Initially my goal was a family, but then I went to college and a degree was what I was after. I couldn't do anything with a B.A. in psychology, so I went into English and taught that for awhile. Then I became a school counselor for several years and got my master's. After realizing the limitations of that, I changed to the business world because I could use some of the skills I'd learned in counseling when dealing with people.

"Basically I see goals in terms of a career, because I've always seen myself as working. I was never raised to get married. I was raised to support myself. That came from my mom. My dad encouraged learning stuff. He got a car and tore it down with me one time so I could know how to do it. Now in a career sense I'm up in the air. But in the personal sense I'm better off than I ever was. I'd like to live in a communal situation and have close people nearby who are bisexual."

"To keep experiencing things that are happening," was Stella's main goal. "People make the world, and if I can reach out and touch them I'll be fine. I want to touch everybody, see everything. Money? I'll have it. It's not like I have to go a certain place, do a certain thing or have a certain amount of money. Whatever happens, happens, as long as I can keep experiencing."

Nearly 90 percent of the respondents felt they were more introspective than average. They replied that they had to be, partially because they were fighting against something so very basic to society by being bisexual. In doing this, they realized they could not simply function but must analyze their actions and emotions. Their lives alienate many. Because they question many of the traditional concepts of our society, they have to reserve time to determine why they set themselves apart.

These women are not inhibited in acting on their sexual orientation. When asked whether this lack of inhibition applied to other aspects of their lives, the answer was a resounding "yes." Ninety-five percent felt that in general they easily flowed with situations. Inhibition is a learned response. Through conditioning people are taught to curb their spontaneity. They are committed to the belief that as long as they are not harming another individual they will do what they want to do.

Are they fulfilled? Yes and no; but the ambiguity stems more from their financial condition rather than their emotional state. It is still hard for an American woman to be economically stable. Job equality is not a total reality. Many of the women originally pursued careers in traditional occupations such as teaching, nursing, and secretarial work, and they were overly qualified for the positions they held. Those in creative fields are comparatively young—in their twenties and early thirties. Professional success is not theirs yet. Most have worked through any upheavals connected with their attraction to both sexes. A few mentioned seeking professional help from therapists, psychologists, or psychiatrists to aid them in coping with problems in their lives, but these were not solely the result of their sexual orientation. Because there was no question as to whether they had ever been hospitalized or under psychiatric care, these factors cannot be considered. Emotionally, the majority perceived themselves as more fulfilled than the norm. But perhaps they would never have granted an interview if this had not been true.

6.

The Pressure Cooker

Striking a course at odds with mainstream American morality is tough. It intimidates the weak, scars even the strong. There is something in all people that cries out for acceptance; something that makes us want to be similar to others. Bisexual women experience inner pressure to bow gracefully and conform. A number of their problems would be simplified by denying their dual sexuality. If their sexual attachments were reserved for men, they would no longer have to hide a portion of their character from those around them who will not tolerate anything but the norm. By declaring interest only in women, they would find solidarity with the gay community. Emotional conflicts could lessen. Support and understanding would be theirs. Yet there is that constant knowledge that this decision would make them untrue to themselves. They cannot snuff out interest in one sex just to please society or gain unity with gay sisters.

In reexamining the dilemmas they encountered when first acting on their attraction to members of the same sex, their uncertainties about whether they are lesbians, and their efforts to clarify their motives and actions, many bisexual women have had to ask themselves some difficult questions. Are they honest in proclaiming an equal capacity to love both sexes?

Why do they turn from men to women and back again: anger, frustration, inability to love either completely—or joy, happiness, an extension of friendship? Are they really in a transition period that ultimately will bring them to exclusive heterosexuality or homosexuality?

Sixty-five percent said they have resolved their internal conflicts about having to make a definitive choice. They were confident with their decision to live their lives as they saw fit rather than succumb to exterior values and the limitations of physically relating exclusively to one sex.

Elaine spoke for many. "I no longer feel under pressure to make a choice. For me it's not either/or. It's always both. I never feel as if I'm rejecting one for the other. This is the way I am with everything, including food, clothes, activities. I continually want to try everything." Ramona responded briefly, "I feel comfortable being bisexual." Brenda said she was past the point of worrying about her sexuality. "It's strictly the mood now. I'll get dressed one night and wind up going to the women's bars rather than the straight bars. Or I'll turn down a date with a guy because I feel like going out with a woman that night. I follow what my biology tells me."

The replies from those continuing to sense confusion ranged from Alicia, who said it was the "major trauma" of her life, to Annette, who described it as an occasional problem. Even though Gretchen lives with a male lover she presented this example of the mental seesaw she rides. "Especially when things with men aren't working out too well I think, 'That's because you're really a lesbian. You really want women. You're just trying to make this straight life work for you.' I sit down and say, 'I'm a lesbian.' And I try to believe it, act on it, but it doesn't happen. So far I have to say I don't think I'm gay. I'm not entirely straight. I'm somewhere in between.

"I think the confusion comes from my disillusionment with the nuclear family and male/female roles, but I see similar problems with gay couples. It's really coupling that bothers me, too, and looking to others for satisfaction instead of to oneself."

Amy talks about conflicts diminishing as the years go by. "When I was younger and first tripped into the whole world of relating with women, I felt upset. I thought that gay or straight were the options. For me there's a real strong feeling—there's something about not wanting to be lesbian in the sense of not wanting to have the hassle. Every once in awhile I wonder where I am with men. Am I sure those feelings are there? I check them out, and I do feel they exist. I'm really glad about that because I don't want to have to make a choice."

Internal pressures that are the direct result of external forces are hard to combat. Unanimously the women stated that if they were left alone to lead their lives without everyone making overt and covert value judgments, their emotions would smooth out. Why is the tradition of the rugged individualist lauded in all facets of character except sexual orientation? There we find continual demands from our basically heterosexual society. Reinforcement of these concepts permeate our culture. Advertisements show two people together, rambling through beautiful scenery sharing a cigarette, dancing until dawn, locked in an embrace —always a man and a woman. Movies, situation comedies, plays, and romantic novels concern the straight existence. Two women together in art, cinema, and literature are lovely to behold but seem to be seen through the eyes of an observing male. When homosexual couples are portrayed, it is not in a positive light.

Although an exclusive heterosexual life-style is held up as the true, the only way, some women believe female childhood conditioning is confusing on this issue. As Carrie pointed out, women's early sex training is "negative and absolutely lesbian." She continued, "When I look back at my sex experiences I realize I was always told, 'Don't do this with *boys,* because boys will think you're bad. Boys will get you pregnant. Boys will talk about you. Boys try to take advantage of you. Beware.' I think a lot of women undergo that. Because boys do all these horrible things, we are unconsciously encouraged to manifest our developing sexuality with other females. It doesn't occur to parents to list all the conflicts that come down on you if you continue to sexually relate to women."

When adult women are asked who they are seeing, this translates to what man or men are in their lives. Marriage is encouraged. Females can proudly display their engagement rings, wedding bands. They are free to discuss male lovers but have to be cautious about confiding about women they love. Barbara described this pressure as subtle but always present. "I feel society saying to me, 'You should be heterosexual.' You go to a concert or on an outing, and everybody is in couples, straight couples. They can do what they want to do, and I can too, as long as I'm with a man. When I happen to be involved with a woman I have to put up with the same bullshit that all lesbians do."

Relating to a man is condoned. But bring a woman on the scene and everything alters. The bisexual women must deal with all the pressures, confusions, and problems with which homosexuals contend. Do they hide the fact they have a woman lover? What happens on holidays—do they always have to be spent without their partner? When expensive gifts are exchanged do they create some charade about its source? How far do they go in restricting public displays of affection? There are countless stories of enduring scathing comments from outsiders when they try to do something as harmless as hold hands with another woman.

Books have been written about these struggles for homosexuals. Yet bisexual women have a unique double pressure situation. They endure verbal assaults and distrust not only from straight women but from gays, as well. With a combination of guilt and embarrassment they mention these direct confrontations, which they feel are almost more psychologically disturbing because they "expect more from other women, expect them to be more sensitive to their sisters' needs, more giving and understanding." But this is not always the case. With a barrage of criticism and disapproval, announced bisexual women have been castigated by the more vocal members of the women's movement and especially by radical lesbians.

Gretchen mentioned all these factors working on her at one time. "I experience a lot of pressure from my mother to find a husband. That's first. My close friends don't bother me, but I feel the general societal pressure. I wouldn't want to be gay, though. I've thought about it when I was in love with one particular woman. What if I wanted to settle down and be with her the rest of my life? Then I'd have to declare myself a lesbian and take all the consequences society heaps on them. I had a nice fantasy of the two of us having a house, living out in the country, and becoming happy old lesbians. But I think I'd rather not. I'd rather continue being the way I am.

"Over the past few years I've felt growing pressure when I'm at women's meetings to kind of pretend I'm gay, not mention my heterosexual side. In fact I've gone to meetings and talked about my relationships with women and my homosexuality and never once mentioned that I'm in love with a man. I'd go home and feel really guilty. Although I didn't lie, I'm sure everyone there was under the impression I was gay. I found it really hard to say, 'But I relate to a man.' The fact that I do has been a secret burden I carry. This political movement of radical lesbians within the ranks of feminists has brought this about. But at the same time, while acknowledging that a lot of women experience that, feel badly about it, it's not as pervasive as the pressure to be straight. Some of it—what the gay women think—is inconsequential in the long run, though it seems important right now.

"Then another time when some straight women learned I'm bisexual I could tell they thought I was some kind of a freak. They didn't know how to deal with me. One kept insisting I had to have a preference because it was unnatural not to. Didn't I really like men better and just get it on with women to gain acceptance from gay women? Or wasn't I really gay, but didn't want to admit it to myself? Their attitudes toward me did an about-face. Previously they'd felt comfortable around me, I'm sure. Then all of a sudden they acted like I was going to drag them off to the bedroom or something.

"Sometimes it's harder for me to deal with that pressure than society's. I don't mind bucking society, but I do mind bucking other women's beliefs."

Being exposed to pressure and learning how to handle it becomes an integral part of these women's lives. Nancy explained her actions and reactions to this conflict. "I've felt pressure from gay women," she said. "Since I've been reading this year, turning off to men's consciousness, I've wanted to find some women to be friends with. For a few months I went to women's bars because that was the only place I could think of to meet women. The ones there were just so conventionally dyke-looking and would push such hostility toward me because I'd come in looking the way they didn't want me to look. A friend of mine who's a lesbian feminist said they probably felt threatened by me and that's why I got such bad vibes. I felt pressure from them that if I wanted to join them to do it, but cut my hair. Come in looking like them. And I won't do that.

"I'll persistently wear make-up to feminist meetings because I don't like that pressure. I just get very rebellious if anyone tells me what I should and shouldn't do. Even if I wouldn't normally do something, I'll do it just to spite the women who are telling me not to. The pressure from straights hasn't been there as much because I don't think they care to the same extent. I guess it's like any movement. In the beginning you've got to be more close-minded. You search for strength through conformity based on your own insecurity. Once you feel good about yourself then you can go about understanding others. Straight people have society's stamp of approval, so they don't get as upset by other's actions. They see me as more straight than gay. I relate to men, and they can deal with that. I'm not abusing them emotionally, and gay women feel that I am.

"I'm tired of the antagonism and fear between women based on our sexual preference. It's just a perpetuation of the same trip we're fighting in role-stereotyping. First women allow men to pit us against each other in competing for them. Some separatist women take all the worst male attributes and then claim all other women are still under the sway of men while they aren't. Some treat straight and bisexual women worse than they treat men. They trust us less. All women should really try and get in touch with their nurturing and love aspects. That's what being bisexual means to me—learning to bend, to find the best in both sexes.

"Now my reaction to these pressures and conflicts is to pattern myself after my archetype Wonder Woman. I really want to be Wonder Woman, with a star on my forehead. Fly around and do it all on my own until things settle down. Have sexual experiences very freely, but not out of this driving need to be completed. I'd like to complete myself and love as equals. That's the solution I'm aiming at."

Judith agreed with Nancy. "Several relationships that I've had which were very short-term were with radical lesbians. They really laid unfortunate trips on me about having to commit myself to the women's movement by not having anything to do with men; by disassociating myself from the real world. I resisted that and still do. I consider myself a very political person. I don't like having someone dictate a policy to me that seems to be unworkable in society, and to me that's what a lot of radical lesbianism is. I feel together about my sexuality and see those women as trying to pick away at my base of security by saying, 'You're with women. Why do you need to be with men?' "

Cindy talked about the pressures she has endured

and resents. "Some of the separatists I know lay these raps on me. They'll say, 'Stay away from men. They're not a positive influence on you.' They resent the fact I'll go to gay bars, but I'll be with men if that comes up, too. I don't like that attitude. Not all men are bad, just the same as not all women are good. To me being gay is as limiting as being straight. And I'm trying to get away from that limitation. We're here. We have numerous possibilities of expressing things and relating to different people in different ways. You can't be lovers with everybody, obviously, but we can experience a wide variety of things. We shouldn't restrict ourselves."

Confrontations with the straight segment of society have not happened to Liz because, as she said, most people assume she is part of their "basket." This has caused both problems and amusing moments for her. "There's pressure but frankly I don't care what anybody thinks," Liz began. "I don't think there's any group who could make me make a choice, because it's not their prerogative to back me into the decision-making corner.

"I went to a women's conference in Los Angeles and was treated with some rudeness because they assumed I was straight. What was I doing at their conference? Well I was giving a workshop, that's what I was doing. Everyone around there was gay, but then they never asked me either. They based their judgment solely on visual appearances, which is something no one should or can do with absolute accuracy.

"I had another experience in New York. An old friend of mine had me in for dinner and drinks with some other people. We hadn't seen each other for fifteen years, and he's grown prejudiced in his middle forties. He hates the black people on Eighth Street and is into calling them 'niggers.' So he leaned toward me at one point and said, 'I'll bet that's what you've done. You've taken a black lover. Tell me, isn't it true?' I knew he was kidding, but there was absolute silence in the room. I said, 'No, she's white.' They were absolutely stunned, because when we go through these labeling things everyone has to think of me as just relating to men. Why that is, I do not know.

"The people reacted by just screaming with laughter, because the line was so good and they were all actors. But then my friend couldn't believe it. He got drunk that night and went on a kind of guilt trip because he's gay and never has been anything else. He said, 'Oh, it must have been something I did when we were in college. I've influenced you into this bad life . . . blah, blah, blah.' It had been so many years since I'd seen him, so it must have been a long, slow take."

In searching for a safety valve to release some of the internal and external pressure, the women often turn to friends. But confiding in friends can be difficult. Most women do not issue a blanket statement; they tell those closest to them in a highly selective manner but wish this were not necessary. While people are not totally defined by their sexual preferences, society singles out this factor for close scrutiny, and bases all sorts of value judgments on this aspect of personality. Therefore bisexual women are often very cautious about confiding this information. A few respondents have talked to only one or two friends. Their greatest concern is the loss of friendship of heterosexual females, whom they perceive as the most judgmental.

All stress that the crux of being bisexual is much more than a sexual issue. It is an emotional, psychological, and social one as well. Being bisexual does not mean they have sexual relations with both sexes but that they are capable of meaningful and intimate involvement with a person regardless of gender.

How do friends handle the knowledge of a bisexual woman in their lives? The reactions of heterosexual men fall into a few basic patterns. After learning that a woman friend is bisexual, some respond with a bland "So what else is new?" or "Aren't all women?" This reaction probably stems from the fact that from early childhood it is acceptable for females to be affectionate toward one another as well as toward males.

More often, the men are intrigued and titilated by the possibilities of relating to a bisexual woman. She is an embodiment of their sexual fantasies about watching two women making love and then, of course, joining them. Many men believe only they can bring a female true sexual pleasure, because they have the right equipment. Viewing bisexuality in a narrow context, their curiosity and desire are aroused by the purely sexual aspects and they ignore the ramifications of the emotional aspects involved.

A corollary to this response can be seen in some men's attitudes toward competing for the bisexual woman. For example, Ramona described an experience she had while in an exclusive relationship with another woman. A former male lover came to town. Even though she explained her situation, he continued to call, visit, and press his attentions on her. It required a great deal of discussion to convince this man that her female lover was as important to her as any man could be. Finally, after he left the city, he wrote Ramona saying, "I really didn't think two women could love each other with the same intensity as a man and a woman. If you'd had an old man I wouldn't have put the pressure on, but since you claimed to have an old lady, I didn't see her as competition."

For other men, difficulties arise because they do not know how to compete. With no ground rules to follow, they are stymied. At least when a woman is seeing other men they have established procedures to guide them in gaining her interest. Few have any experience in this type of triangle.

Another male response is that all the woman really needs is "a good lay"—then she will be back to "normal." They cannot believe that two females can sexually and emotionally satisfy each other.

Many men feel threatened by a woman's bisexuality. They are disturbed by the whole issue of any person relating to members of the same sex; confused by the fact that the woman relates to the opposite sex too, and therefore does not act like a lesbian. She does not reflect all those preconceived stereotypical images they had. Confronting bisexuality in women causes some men to question attractions they might have had for other men and never acted on. It produces a variety of thoughts they do not want to deal with. While trying to sublimate these emotions, they sometimes erupt when a relationship with a bisexual woman is faltering. Instead of assuming some of the responsibility for the failure, they will angrily ascribe it to the woman's lesbian tendencies.

Many of the women feel that with bi- and homosexual men these problems are not likely to arise. They are also living alternate life-styles and can be more understanding. A number of bisexual women believe bisexual men are more aware of relating to the whole person rather than to a bed partner. Bisexual individuals feel a strong affinity through shared experiences. In cases where they have met at mixed bisexual rap groups, the women report these men "restore their faith in *man*kind." They empathize with their experiences. These are men actively trying to comprehend the workings of women's minds and emotions as well as their own. Some even consider these small, tight enclaves as the vanguard in changing attitudes toward sexuality.

Many bisexual women have gay men friends. They report that because sex between men and women can be violent and hostile as well as soft and loving, bisexual women and gay men offer each other companionship without fear. The men provide valuable input to the women's lives minus sexual tensions.

How does a husband respond to the knowledge his wife is bisexual? Again the difference lies in his sexual orientation. Heterosexual men tend to minimize the importance of their wives' extramarital affairs with other women and not consider them threats. All the respondents with straight husbands have been married five or more years. The men generally accept outside relations if they do not jeopardize their primary union. Naturally where the wife's attraction to a woman was intense enough to raise the question of divorce, the husband was forced to consider the other woman a serious rival. In each situation such as this, the wife decided her marriage was more important than an affair and broke with her lover. The men's basic approach has been acceptance as long as it doesn't interfere with them. The majority of these women have not told their husbands they also sexually relate to men outside their marriages. They feel these affairs would be more difficult for their husbands to handle because of the direct competition another man would represent.

Fran described her husband's reaction in this way. "What we've agreed is that I need to do what I need to do, but it will not take from our relationship. My husband is the type who is heavily involved with his work and life and frankly needs a minimal amount of personal contact in a time sense, but a tremendous amount in a quality sense. The time we have together, we both work hard to make it good. Not that we're necessarily always happy, but I mean that we're relating at that time. It's meant some careful planning. His main demand on me is that my outside interests not disrupt our relationship.

"I feel good about the people I'm dealing with because they don't expect me to be exclusive with them in terms of a long-lasting living arrangement. Also, I don't have a pressure build-up in me. I keep thinking of an earthquake fault. These little slippages of pressure make for a smoother functioning in the long run. I release the tension and take care of the sexual needs that I cannot meet with my husband. These factors make for a better me. My husband is not a prince to be held up and admired as a great stoic. His sexuality is different than mine. Perhaps he's having affairs on the side, too. I don't know. What I offer him is a good home and deep love and devotion. If anything, when we're together I give him more than the average wife to make up for my divided energy outside our marriage. And he knows that my loyalties, ultimately, are with him."

For those whose husbands are bisexual there seems

to be less pressure. One partner is a reflection of the other. In most cases this bond of similar sexual orientation drew the people together and continues to add to the marriage. Most of these women said ideally they and their partners would like to establish some form of extended marriage, including another person or persons in their living arrangement. Helen discussed this aspect of her marriage: "My husband and I were fantasizing about our lives. What he brought up and I agreed with was we would like to have a three-way marriage. I would have someone else to help with the children and be a close friend. He would have friendship and emotional support from another woman who made no sexual demands on him. If I had a permanent lover he would like her to live with us. He'd also like to feel that if he had a male friend with whom he was close that he could come and live with us. We also agreed that we very much want to stay together."

Virtually all bisexual women confide in at least a few female friends, although not all are sure about the honesty of their friends' comments. They report that some heterosexual women are accepting. They enjoy the women's company, and this does not alter their feelings. Others are extremely curious. They feel more at ease questioning the bisexual woman than a gay woman because they still have the common bond of sexually relating to men. In some instances they envy the bisexual woman's freedom. They might have wanted to act on their own feelings of attraction but never had the courage or the opportunity.

Sometimes the straight woman feels as threatened as her male counterpart, but for different reasons. She believes the bisexual woman will try to seduce her. She looks for hidden meanings in every interchange, every action between the two of them. Occasionally she may flirt to check the response that elicits from her bisexual friend. Some bisexual women reported conversations or telephone calls from heterosexual women propositioning them. They resent being treated as a sex object by a woman as much as by a man and generally discourage that sort of approach.

Some radical lesbians and separatists are very hostile to bisexual females. They are adversaries. Benetia considered this reaction understandable, though unfortunate. "Radical lesbians are an important part of the women's movement, and I feel very strongly about some of their points. I can see that because I'm married they could construe my actions as just having flings with women under the safety of a heterosexual relationship. I'm emotionally ripping off my sisters is their evaluation, and the gay women are the only ones brave enough to say that. In my case, I don't feel it's true, but for an outsider looking in it might appear that way."

The antagonisms between bisexuals and lesbians are balanced by many close friendships. More often than not the gay women have at one time been intimate with men. They know their reasons for no longer wanting those kinds of relationships while simultaneously sharing that memory.

For many people there is total disbelief that bisexuality exists. Heterosexuals think bisexual means the women are homosexual and occasionally have intercourse with men. Gay people understand the word as categorizing straight women who infrequently become involved with a member of the same sex. The feeling that no one believes them can cause bisexuals confusion and frustration. To compound this problem, Barbara mentioned, "Too often we are then taken solely for our sexuality. Therefore we're after everyone we talk to. Needless to say this doesn't always make for pleasant, relaxing conversations."

The two primary motives bisexual women cited for telling their friends about their sexual orientation are the need for release and understanding and the desire to shock. The vast majority subscribe to the first reason, adding that as a friendship develops it is natural to share more and more personal data. Merlin typified the latter point of view. "There is still a heavy taboo against being bisexual, and I've always liked breaking taboos. It's interesting to see how my friends handle it. Sometimes I offer this fact to people just to jolt them. They seem so snugly secure in their vision of sexuality that it's fun to blow their minds."

When it comes to telling parents rather than peers, the women were generally more cautious and apprehensive. Most felt their parents were very conservative in their views on sexual orientation. Thus approximately 80 percent of the respondents stated they had not revealed this part of their life-style to their parents.

Although they maintain contact with their parents and have a good relationship with them, sexuality is one topic which they feel is off limits. They believe their parents prefer to assume that their unmarried daughters are virgins. They do not want to know for a fact that they sleep with men, let alone with women. The parents are involved in traditional marriages and would not be able to understand or handle the knowledge of their daughters' bisexuality. Because it would hinder rather than help their relationship with their parents, they frequently hide the fact from their families, occasionally confiding in sympathetic brothers and sisters.

Some women fear total rejection by their parents unless their sexuality remains hidden. Other women were less threatened but considered the sexual aspect of their lives purely their own business, not subject to parental examination and approval. None of the women interviewed live with their parents. Some purposely moved away to give themselves added flexibility. Many of those who would like to be able to tell their parents feel it would be selfish and self-serving. They have worked hard to measure up to their parents' expectations, and this one factor would be too detrimental, too difficult for them to be exposed to. The response they envisioned from their parents would be a hand-wringing "where did we go wrong."

Even though they have never verbalized their sexual orientation to their parents, several believe the parents sense some difference and are confused by it because they consider only two alternatives. Not having any concept of bisexuality they conclude their daughters must be lesbians. Other women commented that even though they would not lie to their families if asked directly, this issue has never come up. Their parents' main concern is that their children are healthy and content. What they don't know won't hurt them, so there are many things they do not ask.

Joyce touched on many of these points in explaining why she had not told her parents. "So far I haven't told them, but sometimes I think they must know. Why they don't ask me, I don't know. Why I don't say, 'Hey, listen, there's something that's very important to me that I feel you should hear. . . .' I just can't seem to bring up the subject—but then why should I have to? When you leave home you lead your own life. Why do they care about the specifics of how I exist? If they thought I was unhappy, kept asking if anything was wrong, I might tell them. That would be my opening. But I'm not upset, and they realize that. They're proud of what I'm doing professionally, and they like the friends of mine they've met. When I visit, they're pleased.

"Anyway they couldn't give consent one way or the other. It'd be so self-indulgent of me to get it off my chest and see that they couldn't accept it. I know what would happen. They cannot in this lifetime say to me, 'It doesn't matter,' and that's what I want to hear. I want them to feel as I feel about it, that it's a good, positive life-style. They can't. So I'm silent on the subject, and they match my silence with their own."

While Grace has never issued a formal statement about her sexuality to her father, she thinks he "either knows or suspects." She has been close to him for a number of years, especially since her mother died. Because her father functions best by imposing strict censorship on his awareness, she has remained silent on this topic. "The nature of his consciousness is such that certain things are present, but he's not fully aware of them because he's decided they're unimportant. He's programmed himself into what he's going to think about and what he isn't. Since he divides things into realms of consciousness, he only admits to the full awareness of what he wants to deal with. As far as I'm concerned, he's chosen not to deal with me as a sexual being. Why mess things up, is my feeling."

In spite of the trepidation, those who told their parents found them generally accepting. Some said their parents were still hoping they'd get over it, but they were not as shocked as they thought they might have been. Brenda recalled her mother's response, "Well, you've tried everything else, why not this?" Benetia was surprised and pleased by her mother's reaction. Her motive for confiding this information was purely practical. Benetia's husband was out of town, and she needed someone to watch their child while she met her female lover.

"It really was kind of funny now that I think about it," Benetia said. "The fact that I'm bisexual isn't such a big issue in my life. It wasn't something that I felt I had to tell my mother and merely needed the right moment. I was having an affair with a woman, and I wanted my mother to babysit. At first I just asked her, and she said she had to work the next day so she didn't want to. Finally I just told her, 'This woman is my lover and I want to spend the night with her while I have a chance.' Her reaction was great. It turned out there were many women she'd wanted to get it on with and never had. She wanted to know what it was like. After I told her, she agreed to babysit. That was that. No big thing."

Jackie was more systematic when it came to discussing her sexuality with her parents. She felt it was something she had to do and it would strengthen her relationship with her family. Because she and her father do not communicate on many issues, she turned to her mother with this information. "I started gradually telling my mother about the women's movement and then moved on to homo- and bisexuality. I tried to do this in a very detached manner, trying to sound her out as I went along. I had my doubts for a long time about how she'd cope with it. They live in Ohio and it doesn't cost me much living that far apart to keep up the facade of being straight, but I felt pressure from other gay and bi friends to come out. They said I was being dishonest. I checked my mother out, and she seemed OK with things. I gradually told her more and more until it got to the point I was being completely open. She has told me most of the time she'd rather know what's going on than not know. And I gave her a chance to prove that.

"I really feel better for having told her. The fact I can share what's happening in my life, what's important, is meaningful to me and I think it brings us closer. But I also think my mother is an exceptional person. I wouldn't recommend that all gay and bisexual women tell their families. Sometimes it just isn't worth it."

All the participants reported that they confided selectively, offering edited versions of their sexual life-styles to friends, lovers, and husbands—and occasionally even to parents.

Nearly 25 percent either have children of their own or live in households where they are present, which raises the question of how they approach sexuality in general and theirs in particular with children. The replies include those who are not in direct contact with children, speaking from theory rather than experience, as well as those now bringing up children.

On an abstract level all the women agreed on several points: a warm, loving environment will produce a contented child, and this atmosphere can be created by any number of people of either gender; children should be raised in as nonsexist a manner as possible; the entire subject of people as sexual beings should be examined and discussed freely; sex is a natural function to be experienced for recreation or reproduction, with the value of one not outweighing the other; sex can be an extension of love, or simply a casual, pleasurable experience.

Some women stated they would encourage their

children to be bisexual while cautioning them about society's reaction. Others who responded this way felt that warning the child of probable disapproval would only perpetuate traditional attitudes. Let the youngster assume that loving people for themselves is enough, and perhaps acceptance would be more rapid. If children are given the concept that it is natural to love both sexes, then they can choose whether they want to relate to men, women, both, or even neither. They will know there are alternate forms of sexuality and it is their choice to make.

They would teach the beauty of love between people —not that love is fine between men and women but evil and dirty when the individuals are the same sex. They would encourage children to be true to themselves, instead of cutting off a part of their natures because of fear.

Many of the women say they would not treat sex as if it were the private domain of adults. Children have sexual feelings and concerns as well. If they masturbate, so what? If they discover their children experimenting sexually with other youngsters they would not be shocked or appalled. They, too, did the same thing as children and so cannot condemn it.

These theories are fine but idealistic. Matching actions with words is not easy. The greatest difficulties arise as the children grow older and become targets of disapproval because of their mothers' life-styles. Amy, the mother of two children aged eight and thirteen, is divorced. When she was married no one questioned her sexual orientation. Now she has a female lover, they maintain separate households, and the fallout is staggering. Even though they are discreet, severely restricting displays of affection not only in public but in front of Amy's children, many adults in the neighborhood have rushed in to judge. They have informed Amy that her children are no longer welcome in their homes. They cannot force her to move, yet they hope she will. They feel her life-style is detrimental to her children, their children, and the entire community.

The older child resents his mother because of this. He cannot understand why some of his friends are not available to play. Amy, though bitter that any words are needed, has tried to explain her relationship with her lover to her children. The problem has not been resolved. All she can do is continue offering attention, love, and devotion to her children and hope they will do so in return.

Helen's children are approximately the same age, but she is married. None of the families in her community suspects there is any difference between their home life and hers. Therefore she has not had to deal with the types of problems Amy has. She is there to answer questions when asked but does not volunteer additional information. "Anything they ask me, I tell them," she said. "I have a large uncensored library at home, and they can browse for themselves. They learned to read very early, and occasionally I'll see them looking through a few of the books about sexual matters. I remember one time my daughter was looking at one that had a picture of two women kissing. She didn't ask for any further details, so I didn't offer any.

"As far as my own personal sexuality, the first or second time I went to a bisexuality rap my daughter asked me where I had been the night before. I said, 'I went to a bisexuality rap at the women's center.' She thought that over for a minute and then said, 'Are you bisexual?' When I told her yes, she wanted to know what it meant. I answered that meant you could get interested in either men or women sexually. She said 'Have you had sex with women?' Of course I told her yes. Then she said something about would I tell her more about it. My response was that I'd rather wait until she was a little older because I didn't think she had the experience to appreciate it. I'd tell her anything she wanted to know, but just to tell her about it was rather vague. I said, 'Are you really that interested?' She said, 'No, I don't think so.' We left it pretty much at that. She also knows her father has had periods of being gay. The children have even met one of his lovers. Yet she has very theoretical questions about boys.

"Mainly I try to give them a lot of love. They seem to be happy, well-adjusted children, so I'm not too worried."

Benetia laughed when asked about how she approaches sexuality with her children. "What happens and what I think should happen don't always coincide," she answered. "I have the philosophy you answer any question that comes up, but unfortunately my older daughter's the kind of person who doesn't ask any questions. Therefore I've been horribly disappointed. We just finally got to the point by pure accident when she asked me how babies get inside mothers. She's only five, but even that seems like a long time to wait before wondering about babies. She's seen a baby book and saw the sperm swimming up to the egg, so she wondered how the sperm got there. I tried to use technical terms and answer her directly.

"The opportunity to discuss my bisexuality hasn't come up. I'll just wait and see when it's appropriate. I don't really care whether she grows up to be gay, straight, bi, or whatever, but I'm really curious to see. From all the reading I've done about lesbians, because there's nothing really about bisexuals, they tend to be the oldest children. They have indifferent or ambivalent or domineering mothers who hated their younger brothers—which is how I would characterize myself. I hope she grows up to be bi, because I think that's best."

And the other women agreed with Benetia's concluding statement. The benefits far outweigh the disadvantages. Many feel they have lost little while gaining a tremendous amount from this type of life-style.

Some of the gains are obvious; others, less so. If they were not bisexual they would be eliminating about half the population in terms of total involvement. It is exclusivity—homosexual and heterosexual—they rebel against. They feel gay people are just as limited as straight ones, whom they characterize as captives of our societal programming. They see expanded relationships with women as an absolute plus. By loving other women they increase their self-knowledge. This keener understanding of themselves carries over to their unions with men. As they learn to be comfortable, at ease, and honest with women, those patterns of behavior are transferred to their male/female activities.

As bisexuals they do not have to repress or reconcile a part of their nature. If they are attracted to someone, they can act on it. Bisexuality has increased their knowledge of their own sexuality—not just the technical aspects of what does or does not arouse or bring them pleasure, but a greater appreciation of themselves as sexual beings. As Judith explained, "Being bisexual has enabled me to deal with my own sexuality, to really make it part of my life. That's the way it should be for everybody; it shouldn't be just a function that happens at night in the dark."

They feel their sexual orientation has led them to become stronger and more independent. They have developed a resiliency that enables them to withstand disapproval. This factor, they believe, has made them more empathetic to a broader spectrum of people. Rather than looking for flaws they search for the good in a person. They give others the benefit of the doubt and expect the same treatment in return.

Many view the advantages in purely personal terms. They would have been denying themselves meaningful relationships with specific individuals, and their lives would have gone in different directions if they had not allowed these to occur.

The losses are primarily twofold. The first is the initial confusion they felt when realizing they were moving on to a solitary course. It is much easier to follow the norm. The other disadvantage is similar to those voiced by any homosexual. They regret the restrictions on openly relating and acknowledging love when the person happens to be of the same sex. They cannot proudly proclaim their emotions to all their friends and family. They cannot say, "This is the person I love. Look at her and what we have together, how good we are for each other." Games, charades, and pretenses develop.

Brenda added these comments about what she has gained and lost by being bisexual. "It's given me a chance to see both women and men as equals. I always did when I was younger. I couldn't understand any prejudice that was against me because I was a woman. It never dawned on me the reason some people put me down in certain areas was because of being female. Now I've worked through that. I can once again see women and men both from a friendship and sexual standpoint. It's taught me that the main differences between the sexes are physical.

"The only loss is the time and energy I wasted—not so much in coming to grips with the fact that I was bisexual, but in knowing that I was bisexual. If I had realized it—that yeah, you can be both—then all those years wouldn't have been wasted."

For Grace the losses have been minimal when compared to the tremendous amount she has gained. She believes the major obstacle in many people's lives is their inability to decide what is best for them as opposed to most acceptable in relation to society. This is not a selfish approach but one that results from knowing yourself and then doing something about it. "I'm a better, more honest person because I acknowledge to myself interest in both sexes," Grace said. "I've known a lot of men whom I think really were attracted to other men. I always question my friends to find out what's making them tick, so I'll ask them about this. They'll insist they're not attracted to men and it's not important to them. Yet the way they act seems to indicate to me in so many ways that they are, but they're just so chicken-shit to do it. I don't think they're gay, but the fact they have not had this experience once, fulfilled it, when they have had the attraction cuts them off because they don't want part of themselves.

"They can't make the choice to be or not to be bisexual. They don't know—and that astounds me, not to know something. When you have the chance to experience something for yourself, do it. You aren't hurting anyone, and you have so much to learn. To me it's an overwhelming benefit to be able to be true to yourself. How else could I live with myself if I weren't?

"I also think it's easier for me and women in general to be bisexual. We haven't had our sexuality publicized the same way men have. Women's sexuality is not as attached to our egos. It's a very complex problem. Women have been isolated as sexual beings, totally sexual beings, and that's all. So that's left their spiritual identity really separate and free. Very wrong, very evil and inhibiting in one way, and then very freeing in another because we've been permitted to just operate on different levels. Whereas with a man there's just too much pressure. It's a crazy amount of pressure and debilitates most of the men I know. Whereas I think women have the ability to transcend that pressure a little more easily, so it's better for them. Experiencing both men and women has provided me with insight into myself. I act, rather than react. To my mind those are incredible gains. I wouldn't want to be any other way."

Gretchen captured many women's thoughts when she said, "I don't think I've lost anything that really matters, while I've gained an overwhelming amount of understanding about the workings of my life and others. Yet, at times it's a difficult life-style because I feel alone, but at the same moment I realize it's extremely rewarding emotionally. I think I'm able to love more people more closely, and I don't mean just physically. No one can pigeonhole or restrict me the way they could if I were gay or straight, but I resent society pressuring me to hide a side of me that's so important and worthwhile. Bisexuality is a positive, enlightened force."

7.

Both Sides
Against the Middle?

Do heterosexual and lesbian women react toward bisexual women in the manner described in the previous chapter? Were their emotions and thoughts on the subject of bisexuality correctly evaluated? After questioning a wide cross section of females, targeting those in the same age bracket and with similar backgrounds as the respondents, I was able to gauge their responses with a high degree of accuracy. Curiosity, rejection, intimidation, hostility, interest, disbelief, wariness, distrust, acceptance, shock, denial—all were mentioned. Six women's comments were selected as most typical. Three have been exclusively heterosexual all their lives. Three define themselves as lesbians.

Lucy is a low-keyed, sensitive woman. She was raised on the East Coast, but for the past seven years she has lived in California. After graduating from college she had several jobs before her present one with a large, multinational corporation. Even though she is close to thirty, she is frequently required to show identification proving she is over twenty-one when out drinking with friends.

She has been exclusively heterosexual and is content with that life-style. When asked if she had any positive or negative statements to offer on her relationships with men, she quickly answered, "No, I enjoy men."

She tried to remain as objective as possible but said it was difficult to respond to some of the questions because she rarely thought about her own sexuality, let alone alternate forms of orientation. That admission made her representative of many other straight women.

"I don't have any firm ideas or feelings about bisexual women," Lucy stated, "because before this interview I've never given much thought to anyone's sexual preference. I guess the main thing I believe is to each his own. Every now and then when I'm with my friends someone might bring up gay people, but it's certainly not a normal discussion topic. We're not condemning. It's more not really being able to understand why a person would be that way. As far as I can remember no one has talked about bisexuality.

"I've never felt sexually attracted to another woman, and I'd be very amazed if I ever did. Maybe the thought of getting together with another woman has come to mind, but I haven't dwelt on it enough to actually ever want to enter into it. I'm just not that way. More of my friends are women, and that's where I'd go for emotional support, but men fill an important part of my life. I can't imagine what it would be like not to have them around.

"I'm sure that none of my friends are gay or bisexual; at least none that I know of. The closest I've come is one older woman at work. I've heard from other people that she's that way, but I've never talked to her about it. I never would. I do find it kind of strange. I know I shouldn't be like that, have that reaction, but I do. I'd never stop associating with her, even though I don't have that much contact with her. But it does more or less change my opinion of her. Somehow I can't understand it. What makes a person homosexual or bisexual?

"If a good friend were to come to me and say she was bisexual, I'd find it hard to relate to her. Because something like that has never occurred, I'm only guessing what my reaction would be. I think it would upset me, while at the same time I wouldn't want to judge her or have it alter our friendship. What my mind tells me and my emotions say are very different. My mind says as long as she isn't hurting anyone else, it shouldn't matter. But my emotions—well, I might feel uncomfortable. I wouldn't feel threatened, because it's no direct assault on me or the way I live—but in a subtle way it is. She might force herself on me and make me feel strange. I'd hope she wouldn't think I was the one who was restricting myself, because I'm not. I'm perfectly happy the way I am.

"I've never thought of gay or bisexual people as being mentally ill. It's just the way they are. Like with gays, if they feel that way, then I admire them for following their feelings and not trying to suppress or ignore them. I guess at least I'd have to respect them for recognizing and acting on their needs rather than being miserable and not. But just because they're going against society doesn't mean they're any more liberated than I am.

"In my opinion it would be a difficult way to live, mainly because our nation isn't comfortable around gay or bisexual people. Maybe uncomfortable is the wrong word. Quite frankly I don't think most of us even think about them. Gay people have been getting more attention lately, but who ever thinks about bisexuals? It might just be another fad going around. For a while everyone was into free love. Then everyone was talking about group or open marriages. This might be similar. There'll be a lot of stuff in the news, and then it will die away like everything else."

Mariella, married and the mother of three children, had slept only with her husband until six months ago. As their relationship grew rocky, she had a brief affair. Now they are trying to resolve their difficulties. Their home is a comfortable one in the suburbs. Although they have a hefty mortgage she has never worked, because she considers it important to be with her children during their early years. Mariella's consciousness about her own sexuality is just beginning to develop. Of all the influences on that aspect of her life, she believes the church was the harshest in its teachings.

"It's incredible what I was told about sex by the nuns and priests. 'Don't sit on a boy's lap unless you have a telephone book between you.' 'When you dance, don't get too close.' I've just become aware of the heavy trip with my attitude toward sex—not being able to show that I really enjoyed it because then I was losing control. The whole time in school when we were dating we were told, 'You girls are in control. You're the ones responsible. It's the girl's job to keep a man from being turned on. You don't tease.' But the problem was they didn't tell us what turned him on. They didn't even let us know *what* got turned. I was afraid constantly, and because of that I got the reputation of being very cold. All I was trying to do was take care of me and them, too, but not knowing what I was doing. It's taken all these years to overcome that and even see that in myself. Seeing it and dealing with it has helped me become much more free with sex."

Mariella had close girl friends in elementary school but had never been infatuated or sexually interested in another woman. Asked if she had any preconceived ideas about bisexuality she answered, "If I let myself go, I immediately think about homosexuality. I'm not that familiar with bisexuality. It's something that I heard about only a little while ago. Men are what come to mind. I've always associated it with them, probably because no one ever talked about women. To be honest, it wasn't until the past year that I feel my friends have started discussing sex at all.

"I guess a person who's bisexual is someone who could do it both ways with both sexes. I don't really care what people do as long as they're not interfering with me. It's fine with me if my friends are doing it, too. It's just like taking dope. They can do it around me, but don't force me to do it. I've never considered a bisexual life-style for myself. Sometimes I have a hard enough time getting through my heterosexual existence without complicating matters more. It's funny, but just today my girl friend and I were talking about lesbians. I was saying I really like going to bed with a man. I like the different feel of the body, the totally different body—having a penis inside me rather than some phoney thing or having oral sex all the time. I like feeling a man's chest and I can't imagine having somebody else's breasts on top of mine. I really like a man.

"Maybe I've been a little curious of what it would be like, but it's the same way I've sort of wondered about homosexuals. Why would they find it better doing it with someone of the same sex? That's about the extent of my curiosity.

"None of my close friends or even acquaintances are lesbians or bisexuals. It's just been recently that one or two of them have told me that they've even known a lesbian. I've never known any. I've met a couple of homosexual men lately. I get along great with them, and they're real honest about their relationships with other men. I have a friend who just found out he was gay, and he's really fighting it. I've just been giving him a lot of support. 'If you're gay, be gay. Enjoy it. Why fight it?' That's what I've told him. Some friends who know gays and bisexuals have told me about the trips they've gone through because of it. I guess what I'm driving at is all this is very new to me. I don't know if I've lived in a sheltered environment, but it isn't anything I've come in contact with much. Mainly I have to worry about taking care of the house and my kids. After I had that affair and all the problems that brought out, I did think more about sex. I also realized it can be a lot of fun. Since I'd only been to bed with one man in my life, the person I married, I didn't have anything to compare it with. I know I'd come a long way since we'd first gotten together, but it took so long for me to relax and enjoy myself.

"I'd be surprised if any of my good friends came and told me they were doing it with another female. Like my best friend is just crazy about men. I'm trying to picture what that scene would be like. I don't know.

I'd hope to say, 'That's great,' but I'm not sure. It wouldn't turn me off to her at all. I think the first re-action would be that when she hugged me the next time I'd sort of think, 'Oops.' I'd have to get over that, and it would take a little bit of time to do it. We'd probably sit down and talk about it, and everything would be fine.

"I don't even have any idea how prevalent bisexual-ity is. I really haven't thought about it. I imagine there'd be a lot more if society didn't put its foot down on it, or if people would separate themselves from fear-ing it. The only way things will ever change is if enough people just keep doing what's good for them. And openly doing it, and letting others know that they're not bad. They're not perverted. They're not weird. They're not going to harm anybody, because all it is is people's fears keeping them from seeing people as they are. They're afraid of it happening to them, so they make perverts out of the other people. They're afraid that they might have to look at themselves and think, 'Well, maybe I'm like that, too.' So they just get angry. If everyone would stop being angry, then we'd get it together.

"I'm just really glad that people are finally opening up about sex. Everyone's getting a lot freer on this subject. I'm so tired of all those who take sex so god-damn seriously. I mean, sex is the ultimate bullshit. It is so overrated and publicized in the wrong way. Sex is part of life. Sex is very funny. It's very funny to look at, to see. And it can be very, very intimate, very close. It can be enormous amounts of fun. I'm sick of people trying to make a weapon out of it all the time. Sex isn't a tool that you use on someone else when you want to get something. It's just part of a much bigger scheme of things.

"Emotional help is as important between two people. I push to get that with men because I really feel they have the right to be emotional and haven't had the opportunity to do that. They need support, and the only way they can have that is for me to let them know it's OK. It goes both ways, too. I shouldn't have to go to my girl friends every time I want to let my hair down. Men won't ever change if we don't help them. We have to give them the chance and show them we're willing to let them be the way they want to be. I'm heterosexual, and so that's where I put my time— into making those relationships work. Maybe bisexual women do, too. I don't know.

"I really feel each of us has male and female in us, and we should let all that out, and function on those levels. I find that men can at some times fulfill my emotional needs. It's hardest for my husband, because he's with me all the time. It's most threatening for him to do so. With other men in my life, it's not as much of a threat because it's easier for them to offer me short-term comfort and aid. Some men can do that; some can't. I couldn't rely on any one to do it all.

"I think it's possible for people to love both sexes because of the male and femaleness in us all. I don't think anyone really knows why we are the way we are sexually. Each person has a different place to come from. Like some people just come from a really hurting place. They've had it with the opposite sex, so they'll try the other way. Maybe some women have been so disillusioned and abused by men that they give up on them and become lesbians. They might have been raped or just had enough men dump on them so they say, 'That's it, never again.' Or maybe they had really horrible fathers or brothers. Really I can understand a little better getting rid of one sex completely for whatever reasons. I'm not quite sure why people would go to both sexes. Maybe they've had good experiences with everyone, or they aren't crazy about either. I can see where parents would have a big impact on how a child was brought up sexually and the child's feelings about men and women. There are so many small things that go on in the homes, it would have to affect them.

"I try to approach sexuality completely openly with my children, but with a few restrictions. For one thing, I don't particularly feel like having sex in front of them. That's going too far, in my opinion. If they ever walked in on us, I'd certainly sit down and explain that everything was all right. As best as possible I'd let them know what we were doing and why; that when two people love each other, what they saw was one way of showing it. Right now my four-year-old son is going through a stage where he's really enjoying feeling his body. He takes his clothes off all the time. When I walk in on him, he'll look kind of guilty, which really annoys me. Where did he pick up the guilt? I'll say to him, 'If you want to take your clothes off, it's fine. You don't have to look guilty. What's happening that you feel guilty about?' He doesn't want to talk about it. Sometimes I've noticed him playing with his penis. I just look at him and say, 'That feels good doesn't it?' He goes, 'Yeah.'

"He's in nursery school, and maybe he was playing with himself and the teacher criticized him. It's hard. You try to raise a child not to think that his body or sex is bad, and then the rest of society leaps in and messes up all that you're trying to do.

"The oldest one asked a lot of questions when I was pregnant with the baby. Now he's got it all worked out how babies come. I'm trying to do the best I can. I don't want them to feel the guilt that I did, but it would probably bother me if one of them grew up to be homosexual or bisexual. Then I'd come up with the old standby, 'What did I do wrong?' I'd have to overcome that. Then I'd probably be thinking that there was something I did that caused them to be like that. All your good thoughts go down the drain when it happens to your own children.

"I can allow others the freedom to do what they want, but I'd hate to think it was my fault my kids turned out anything but heterosexual. It's not that I have anything against other ways of doing it, but every parent wants what's best for his children. And it's certainly simpler if they are straight. Maybe by the time they're adults things will have changed. Then it might be unusual not to be bisexual, but I don't see things moving that quickly. We might get even more relaxed about sex than we are now, but I think heterosexual is what people were intended to be.

"Now that I've thought about some of these things, I can see my answers are mixed with opposing comments. I'd like to think that everyone has the right to live their own lives. I'll be interested to see what happens, if there are more stories or discussion about bisexuality. Maybe if I bring that up with my girl friends, they'll surprise me with their answers. I might frighten them. I'll see."

Since Karen's introduction to sexual intercourse at the age of seventeen, she has been exclusively heterosexual. Now twenty-seven years old, she defines her sex life as active. Although she has been involved in a monogamous relationship for the past two years, prior to that there were many men in her life. While sexually sophisticated, her immediate reaction to my questions was in terms of polarities.

"When I hear the word 'bisexual,'" Karen began, "I think of two people of the same sex making love. Just after I said that I realized that is more a definition of homosexuals than bisexuals. It's hard for me to separate the two. Intellectually, I know that bisexuals relate to both sexes, but the picture I have is of a homosexual couple.

"The next image I have is a personal one, two close women friends who are presently lovers, but are bisexuals. A lot of my feelings, concepts, and value judgments will be swayed by my thoughts of these friends. They have such a good relationship that I see it as a positive thing. In general I think that bisexuality is kind of neat, because it's good to experience many different things—and that's one I haven't done.

"I remember two times when I've felt attracted to other women. The first time was about seven years ago, and my reaction was surprise. It didn't faze me much one way or the other. I just saw it as something interesting more than anything else. The second time was about a year or so ago, and by then I was more curious. I thought it was fun that I should see another woman and have a few of the thoughts that wander through my head when I see a good-looking man.

"I didn't do anything about it. In the first situation the other person would have been shocked and amazed. Plus I probably wouldn't have done it, because I'm too inhibited. Somehow I can't see myself sashaying up to some woman and saying, 'Hey, baby, wanna go home with me tonight?' Once I got her home, what would I do? I don't even know what I'd do if someone approached me, so I'm sure I wouldn't come on to somebody else. I might let the idea go through my mind, but that would be the end of it.

"Because some of my good friends are bisexual, I must admit I've thought about that type of life-style, but more on a mental level than an emotional one. Although thinking about it is probably derived from emotions. Often I feel very dissatisfied in a heterosexual relationship—not sexually, but emotionally. Then I question whether I should try getting together with another woman. That might be much easier. Men, or at least most of the ones I know well, seem to be so incapable of discussing feelings. They want to deal with practicalities. 'Well today I had a hard day at work, or school, or life.' Then they list the things they did while I wish they'd open themselves up more and say, 'This is where I'm coming from. This is how I feel about our relationship. This is what's going on in my head at this moment. I don't know what all of it means, but I want to share it with you and together maybe we can find some answers.' But most men won't. Whether they're afraid to show their emotions because of some macho image or whatever reasons, they don't like to reveal themselves or are unable to let themselves go.

"Once or twice I've gone as far as trying to visualize what it would be like to make love to another woman. I'm a woman, but sometimes I feel as if I know so little about my body or those of other women. From the time they're little kids, boys see each others' genitals in communal bathrooms, showers, and so on. I took physical education, I went to slumber parties, yet I don't remember actually sitting down and comparing bodies. I don't know if my vagina is average, large, or small. It didn't even occur to me until a couple of years ago that of course those sizes vary as much as the size of penises. Maybe I'm a freak—I don't have the slightest idea. Whether or not all women 'taste' the same is another thing I'll probably never know. Breasts are somewhat different because they're more obvious. I can't imagine, at least right now, getting together with a bunch of women friends and checking each other out.

"After I thought about getting it on with someone of the same sex, I had to admit to myself that it didn't turn me on. It's just not for me. But I'd like to believe that I'm capable of any change, so I don't totally reject the idea. In my estimation there are more attractive women than men, but I'm not sexually attracted to them. Maybe that's just because I repress it. I couldn't say. It's a possibility for me to be bisexual, but not a probability.

"I can still recall when a couple of my friends told me they were bisexual. The first time I was only twenty-two, and a woman I hung around with brought it up in a conversation. It wasn't like a tremendous announcement, but something she mentioned in passing. I thought, 'Far out, how interesting.' Then she started to tell me about other friends of hers. I probably even thought it was interesting because it was different. At that time I was into being different. I was superhippy with long hair, bizarre clothes, and few aspirations except to be unique.

"The other time was two years ago, and I think my main reaction was I got a big smile on my face. Actually it was before this woman had gotten together sexually with the other woman, but she told me she was turned on by her. The reason I was amused was she was the same person I'd noticed and thought was physically appealing. I could easily see how my friend could be interested in her. When they started doing a thing, I think I was somewhat surprised mainly because my friend had always been heterosexual. She's been married and then had a few other men in her life. Before that she'd never even mentioned anything about the possibilities of bisexuality for herself. It wasn't a shock for me, but I'm probably past shocking. There are so many different kinds of people around nowadays that I don't think much of anything would shock me.

"After she told me I don't think my feelings toward her changed in any way. She'd been my friend for a couple of years, and I couldn't see turning my back on her or yelling, 'Get out of my life, you shameless person.' Whenever we'd see each other we'd still hug, because we'd always done that. I would have been disappointed with myself if I'd started thinking, 'Aha, she's coming on to me. That hug means something much more than it did a few months ago.'

"There was one minor thing that did come up, though. I remember once, shortly after she told me, she and her lover were in my bedroom and I had to change clothes to go to work. For one second something flashed on me. I guess I might have been a little uncomfortable, but then I discarded that emotion. I figured it was no big thing and went ahead and changed clothes. What could I have done anyway? Walked into the next room to change? Then I applied my reaction to another situation. Here she was with her female lover who was basically interested in women. Was she looking at me from a sexual standpoint? What if she had been her male lover? Would I have changed clothes in front of a man who might be putting out the same kind of sexual vibes? Since it was so easy to discard any feelings and go ahead and change clothes in front of a woman-identified woman, why would I hesitate in front of a woman-identified man? I haven't really answered that question for myself yet.

"Then I tried to analyze my feelings towards my

friends. Did it change my relationship with them in any way? I decided it didn't really, but it made them a little more interesting. I don't think I envy them their freedom, because they probably have hang-ups just like anybody else. They just show in other places. Sexual freedom doesn't always correspond to other parts of their lives. They could have just as many problems as I do.

"You know, just by thinking of the people I know, I believe bisexuality is much more prevalent than anybody realizes. When it was more taboo, you thought there were hardly any gay people in our country. Now that it's not quite as taboo, you see so many. And the majority are very attractive people. It's not like they are the physical outcasts of society where all the gay women are dykes carrying chains around and all the gay men are supereffeminate and swish when they walk. That's not the case, in my opinion.

"When I was twenty-one I went to some gay bars with my boyfriend. At lot of the women looked real dykey, but there was one who was extremely pretty. She looked like what I thought of as a 'normal' woman. I remember being surprised. I couldn't believe she was gay, because she looked just like my friends. Now I'm seeing more and more gay women who are very beautiful. And also there's no way to tell now, either. You can't tell because of appearances, the way that everybody used to claim they could do. 'Hey, I can always spot a queer.' There are still some obvious ones, but more seem to melt into a normal kind of physical appearance.

"I tend to agree that we are all bisexual by nature. It's a learned response to be heterosexual. I think the more natural way to be is if we really care for someone to show them physical as well as verbal affection. It's so normal and accepted to reveal physical affection to a member of the opposite sex, put an arm around his shoulder, give him a little kiss—but when it comes to people of the same sex, we hold back. It doesn't make sense when it seems like such a natural thing to do.

But I'm part of it. I still save the sexual side of myself exclusively for men even though it does seem illogical and pointless.

"Basically I have a lot more women friends than men. I find men are very unsatisfying emotionally. I think it's just because of the way women have been brought up; it's more acceptable for us to deal with our emotions than it is for men. And men are losing out. Therefore a woman dealing with a man is losing out. Yet there's always something holding me back from a total woman-to-woman relationship.

"When I think about society's impression of bisexual women, I get pissed off. We are a male-oriented, male-dominated society—and by that I mean straight men. It's frustrating to see average straight men's reactions to a bisexual woman. They feel all the woman needs is a good screw from a far-out guy and it will set her straight. She'll see what she's missing all this time. It just knocks me out. Women in general and bisexuals in particular are not a threat to them. They find it intriguing and a challenge for them to 'help' all these pretty women.

"I can see that some super-straight women don't even think about bisexuality. It's not their fault that they haven't had the time or interest to look around. Maybe it's because I've done more things, been with different types of people, that I'm more aware of varying kinds of sexual orientation. Lesbians might be more understanding, because they have probably done both, too. They've probably been to bed with men at one time during their lives. They've been through the trauma of telling their friends they're gay, so they can identify with the bisexual woman.

"I think one of the reasons more and more women are turning to other women as well as men is because it's easier. They get both emotional support and physical enjoyment. I know, and I'm sure every straight woman does, how hard it is to get around to telling a man what to do in bed. It took me ten years before I was able to do that without feeling like an idiot. 'Hey, you're doing it in the wrong place. This feels good. A little more to the left. That's called a clitoris. It likes a lot of attention.' It's amazing how many men do not know what to do. It's certainly not their fault. If nobody ever tells them what to do, how are they supposed to know? Women are brought up totally differently from men as far as sex is concerned. We're told it's a nasty thing and we're not supposed to do it. We're supposed to save it for our husbands. All those little things that have fucked us all up. You'd never have to tell another woman what to do, because she already knows. So in that case it would start out just being a freer thing sexually, so it wouldn't be as inhibiting in certain ways.

"With men you have to work through all your inhibitions before you can overcome your fear or whatever it is and tell them what brings you pleasure. In that way I can see how it's really simple for women to get together physically, if they get over that basic reaction that it's a horrible thing for two women to make love.

"People make a much bigger deal out of men being gay or bi than women. It's because women are more affectionate to begin with. When you see two women kiss in public, not passionately, but even on the lips, others aren't inclined to go immediately, 'Oh, they're gay.' But when men do that, instantly, 'They're gay.' Although women have been raised to devote themselves to men, they've also been taught to express their emotions. Everybody's had girl friends when they were growing up whom they've kissed or hugged. It's a more natural thing for two women to get together than two men. With a man there'd have to be something more overt about his life for him to become gay. Whereas with women it almost seems like a natural course. I also think women are more prone to bisexuality than exclusive homosexuality. I bet there are many more bisexual women than gay. Since we have been taught to show our emotions, there isn't as much of a conflict, and we are allowed to reveal them to both sexes.

"What I feel is kind of ironic is women have been held up as sex objects for everybody and now more women are getting off on them too. It might serve men right, if all the women became gay and said, 'We don't need those men.' Maybe we could have a few sperm banks. Then when the men ask us why we've left them, we could say, 'Well you've been showing us those pictures of these lovely women all through the years, and we finally caught on. You were right all the time.' I think bisexuality is a viable lifestyle, but it's still not for me."

Dale, twenty-seven, is the oldest of three children. When she was thirteen, her family vacationed with another family. She and their daughter spent that week in sexual exploration. It distressed Dale to the extent that she never saw her friend again. At twenty-one she had intercourse with a man entirely out of curiosity. All her life she has been attracted only to women. The three men she slept with were to relieve boredom or satisfy inquisitiveness. For political and emotional reasons she classifies herself as a lesbian, yet the majority of her life she has been self-sexual. If she were to sexually relate to another person, she would turn to a woman. At present she has not found an individual she cares to see on a regular basis. Using free association, Dale defined a bisexual in two ways: "A baby who is sexual and hasn't yet been programmed one way or the other; adults who, for whatever reasons, don't have political or emotional motives behind their sexuality that put them to one side or the other."

She believes she does not have any fixed ideas about bisexual women, because until recently she has not considered this form of sexual orientation. While some acquaintances have now confided that they are bisexual, she totally rejects the possibility for herself. "As far back as I can remember," Dale said, "my whole focus has been on women. Obviously I wasn't part of the women's movement when I was a kid because, among other things, it didn't amount to much. One of the times I went to bed with a guy was because I was in Florida and tired of watching television with my mother. It seemed like one step above that on the scale of things to do to keep from going nuts. It sure wasn't much more than that.

"The concept of bisexuality is fine, because if I can project into the years to come, long after I've expired from this life, it could be the norm. When people get off all their horses, ignore their egos and all their bullshit, it just might work. Women's sexuality in particular has been validated as existing only recently. Therefore it's more discussed, and people are discovering there're more and more options. They're able to see they have choices and are better able to make them.

"I don't think our sexual orientation is genetic except that we're born sexual. Then the society we live in, the environment, our personal style, the 'I,' all determine how we'll express that sexuality. Unfortunately, society has a pretty tacky approach to women and our sexuality. Every now and then I feel especially sorry for bisexual women. They get the worst of both worlds, and I know it. They're pushed out of the straight world for being half queer, and they get shut off from the gay community for not coming out yet. 'Why don't they get their act together' is the feeling many of my lesbian sisters have about them. For bisexual women it's like being the only black in a white crowd. They stand out and have no solid place to go for comfort.

"Sometimes I think this is their own fault. They've got to learn to be completely up front with the women they relate to. The men don't make that much difference to me and shouldn't to them. If they're in the space of relating to another woman and they don't make it clear they're bisexual, then that's a rip-off as far as I'm concerned. Especially if the lesbian is leaning toward separatism or is a separatist. They are not being fair to their sisters. I believe you lay your cards out. If it's clear, then the dyke has the choice. She can stay with the bisexual woman or she can cast her aside.

"I think it's possible for anyone to be bisexual. Even my sister who's straight has gay fantasies she's at ease with, which I think is great. We've all got a bit of everything. There's no one who's pure white or pure black. If it comes out in fantasy or is expressed in reality, it's the same thing. The people toward the middle of the spectrum are called bisexual. And they're stuck in the middle. Right now I'm more concerned with my problems and the concerns of gay activists to really care about them.

"After thinking about the whole issue of women's sexuality for awhile, I believe if the movement is successful and true feminism gets underway, sexuality will not be a question. We'll get down to just people as people. I'm more of a humanist, and I'd like to see those principles more heavily reinforced. If I try to tie someone in with my theories, that's invalid. If I went to another culture, tried to impose my principles on them, and then judged those people according to my culture while in theirs, that wouldn't be right. What we've got to learn to do is judge people on how they judge themselves.

"If someone has his or her set of principles, is functioning under them and not fucking over anybody else, then there's no reason to bother them. Except maybe if they get into goldfish or something weird like that. But if the fish don't mind, it should be all right. Let people be. That's cool. You've got to cut loose from those feelings of trying to make everybody be like you are. If everybody was like I am, I'd be bored out of my mind. I wouldn't have to talk to anybody. We'd just be robots.

"It would be a better society if we didn't define anybody sexually, but that's impossible right now. The way we culturally stand, people seem to think it makes a difference. Personally speaking, 95 percent of my life I'm self-sexual. Politically I'm defined as a lesbian because at this point it's necessary for me to make that statement. My sexuality isn't anybody's godamn business, but my politics are. That's why I've made this type of declaration to those around me, those who play an important part in my life. I'm saying, 'I'm with you. I'm a feminist. I'm a lesbian who's working for the cause of freedom.'

"What I wonder is when this world is going to get its act together and stop fucking with people. It's ridiculous. My brother's a sexist pig hippy. He doesn't know that, because he's ecstatically happy. He's a loving person, but I could never live the way he does. My sister went to college, got married, had kids, taught school. She's happy. I could never do it. What should I do, tell them to be gay? They aren't telling me to be straight, thank God.

"I've met a few men who are really trying to be people, so I don't write off half the population as fuckers. To me it's dumb, but I can understand women who are into separatism. I can understand women who hate men because they've been messed over. But I can't condone it. They aren't going to get anywhere. What they're going to do first is start killing the men, and next they're going to kill each other. I refuse to participate in that.

"I don't feel hostility toward women of other sexual orientations. When I meet someone I don't ask if she's a dyke. If the person's putting out good juice, six months later you meet her lover, you find out what she is . . . maybe. I'm more of a humanist as I said, but my politics are definitely lesbian. I don't relate to men. I have one man I know whom I feel I can approach. He provides me with a little touch into the male mind, which is all I need. It's not all that interesting to me. Gay, straight, bi, I don't care, as long as they don't judge me and try to convert me one way or the other."

Carolyn, twenty-eight, is the only child of a union laborer. Beginning at the age of sixteen, her first sexual experiences were with women. Even though she has been physically intimate with a few men, for the past seven years she has related solely to women. Since receiving her master's degree in social work, she has supported herself by conducting classes and workshops primarily for feminists and women's collectives.

She knows the advantages and disadvantages of being a lesbian. On the emotional side, this aspect of her life has been rewarding. From the practical standpoint, her sexual orientation cost her her last teaching position. The director of the school fired her when he learned she was gay, because he felt she had a distorted view of reality.

At present Carolyn is dividing her commitments between two women. Monogamy, in her opinion, is an unwanted limitation. She states this belief to the women she becomes involved with; thus she finds minimal problems stemming from this facet of her relationships. She began our interview by saying she felt being bisexual would be "difficult and a little strange." When asked why, she answered, "It would be an uncomfortable split or dichotomy in a bisexual's life. Maybe I'm imposing my personal feelings on the topic, but to me it would be strange to live that kind of life. I'd perceive the transition from men to women as very confusing.

"I've pretty much rejected bisexuality for myself, because if I were ever to relate to a man it couldn't be the usual type of experience. It would be something defined by my own needs and not by a social definition of how a man and woman interact. There'd have to be emotional equality in the relationship, and I think that would be difficult to find with most men. It would take a really unusual one. Not only do I require emotional equality, but power and control equality as well. Also there's the fact that I'm interested in people from a more feeling component rather than an intellectual component. Most men wouldn't meet that criteria for me.

"I've had personal experience with bisexual women, beginning with my first lover, who is married. We're still occasional lovers, even though we don't see each other very often. I knew when I entered into a relationship with her there would be a real time limitation on us. This was something I had to deal with. I didn't consider her husband as competition—instead I saw him as a person who also required energy from her. Because she is bisexual, my feelings toward her didn't alter, since it was a part of our relationship from the onset.

"It did make me think about bisexuality more. With my work I come in contact with a great diversity of people. I think that bisexuality is more prevalent than anyone would have us believe. Personally I believe it's a positive life-style, but politically it isn't. When you say you are bisexual, at present, that's no kind of a statement. It's almost as if you were searching for acceptance from everyone; in reality, you find distrust from all sides.

"When I consider the broader picture, I think women in general—and by that I mean the housewives, secretaries, and so forth, those not identified with the women's community in any way—don't define themselves according to their sexual orientation. They just don't even think about homosexuality, let alone bisexuality. They may do it, but they don't give it a title or label. Starting out with the president of the United States down through to middle America, those in suburbia, those who are most concerned about making ends meet, getting through the day without some disaster coming down on them—sex still isn't talked about that much. I'm a political lesbian, so my sexuality has been and is an issue. But most people don't even realize there is such a person as a gay activist. Now if you try to bring up bisexuality, they'd probably throw their hands in the air and say, 'What are you talking about. Ya mean there're more weirdos? What's bisexual anyway?'

"More problems arise when you start approaching those participating in the women's movement. They're more aware of what's happening in all regards to women. When some lesbians come in contact with bisexual women, they think bisexual females are copping out. Bisexuals are hiding out behind the protection of a man or men. There's a real fear on bisexual women's part of taking on a lesbian identity. By that I mean making an open declaration of that sexual orientation, being ready to live with society's hostility. You must be prepared to stand up and be counted on vital gay issues. You've got to support your sisters. As you become more involved, you learn you can't put up with the public's image of lesbians. Some radical lesbians may embarrass them if they look too similar to that image, but you've got to remember they might have had to fight the hardest battles. They don't conceal their sexuality. Maybe the bisexual women feel the dyke and her blatancy is detrimental to the greater purpose, but they must understand where she's coming from as well. You have to counter the lesbian stereotype with challenges to society's thoughts, which are always emotional on this issue. Think of all those things tied up with being gay, and it scares away a lot of people.

"Many bisexual women are probably closet homosexuals who don't have the courage to admit it to themselves. Then they come breezing into the lesbian community and expect support. Well, they can get it because they are women, but at the same time they should be honest in stating why they are there. Are they afraid of being totally identified with our community? Do they publicize the portion of their lives that they relate to women when they are around gay women, then do a flip-flop around straight women and talk about the men they love? I think we question them because we are unsure about their honesty. Some seem to be taking advantage of other women. They want to reap the rewards of being both gay and straight while escaping from the battles we must wage.

"I do empathize with many bisexual women. Some genuinely love the man they're relating to and are confused when they want to relate to women and they aren't accepted with open arms. Others find great solace being with women and troubles when trying to deal with men. I need thinks accurately stated in my head and my life. They should try to do the same. They've got to learn to be honest with themselves before they go running back and forth between both sexes. Intellectually I feel bisexuality should work, but go back to emotions and I wonder if it's completely feasible."

Beverly, the older of two children, was raised in the Chicago area. After completing three years of college, she quit school, first to work and then to travel. She has lived in Japan, Germany, and several different cities in the United States. Through phone calls and letters she tries to keep in touch with her parents, who know nothing about her sexual orientation.

Her income is over eighteen thousand dollars a year, and she smiled with a touch of embarrassment as she pointed out her new color television. "I'm becoming so middle class. My friends don't know how to respond to me any more. Here I am surrounded by my material comforts. I don't look very radical."

After seven years of exclusive sexual intimacy with women, during six of which she was involved in a monogamous relationship, Beverly had an affair with a married man. She became pregnant and had an abortion. "I'd never used birth control because I didn't have to when I was with women. I discovered there's no good way of birth control. I always seem to learn the hard way."

Up until then she had been very active in the lesbian community and had helped organize an ongoing gay support group. Her attitude has changed because of this last year. She had first hand knowledge of the reaction of her gay friends. It made her more understanding to the plight of bisexual women. Even though she had that experience with a man, she continues to declare herself a lesbian with a "temporary lapse of sanity." As she nears her thirtieth birthday, Beverly has no desire to begin another relationship with anybody. She wants to remain detached for a while and analyze her feelings, before trying to resume stronger bonds with another individual.

"I think we should clear up one point," Beverly

said, "I have called and viewed myself as a lesbian for many years. In a utopian society I'd like to think that bisexuality was the best way to go, but too many other issues have to be taken care of first before we'll even come close to that. Right now people have too many hang-ups, men are too vindictive, and roles are too heavily ingrained for bisexuality to be a universal reality. I had an affair with one man, but that doesn't mean I'm bisexual. Most lesbian women have slept with a man or men somewhere along the line, but our self-concept is what's important.

"I didn't turn to a man because I was unsatisfied with women. My relationship with my lover was degenerating. She spent so much time with her work, which was totally different from mine. We had a lot of other problems, which don't matter for the purposes of this interview. I looked elsewhere for affection. I think at the time if there had happened to be a woman who had come into my life, I would have chosen the woman. But looking back at it, I can see I needed someone and he happened to be handy. My relationships with women are much more rewarding than those with men. Since I can see myself continuing to be attracted to women, I'm still closer to being gay. But what that experience did was make me more compassionate to bisexual women. I had some bad moments with my gay sisters that I wouldn't want any person to go through.

"Their reactions shocked and surprised me. Some of my lesbian friends were furious with me. Not only was I with a man, but a married one. They saw that as being even worse. I wasn't respecting them or the man's wife. Territoriality was the issue. My God, how could I do this. One of my friends who came down hardest on me was screwing around behind her lover's back. I tried to correlate the two, but she said there was no comparison at all. My straight women friends who knew what was going on projected the attitude, 'You're getting better, Beverly. You're coming out of your sickness.' Wow, if having to endure an abortion is getting better, I'm not quite sure what getting worse would be.

"I also learned from my experience that the average straight man thinks he can cure you. Either that or he doesn't want to deal with you at all because you're getting more support and love from other women.

"Before any of this happened and I was just going along in my happy, little gay world without any of these confrontations, I learned that some of my other friends were bisexual. They never exactly sat down and told me in so many words, but they expressed their feelings about sexuality in general. I might have been a bit hesitant or guarded because I was so clear about my decision of loving only women, but now I obviously understand much better. I hope it didn't change my feelings about them. I don't remember any of the violent reactions that some of the lesbians had toward me.

"Now that I've done more thinking, I believe there are a tremendous number of bisexual women in our society. Any estimate under 15 to 20 percent is way too low. Although none of my lesbian friends have come to me and said they continue to relate to men but keep it quiet, this might be happening, too. It might not be as evident or open in Fresno or Keokuk, but bisexuality is in the larger cities. In New York City nobody pays that much attention to you anyway. I could run around with a placard covering my whole body declaring my sexual orientation, and no one would even bat an eye. In San Francisco everyone is into something different, so there's not as much question about alternate forms of anything. Chicago is a man's city. There they are too busy trying to make money to think about anything else, so you've got the go-ahead to do what you want with pretty much freedom.

"When the total society stops to think about bisexuality, they'll probably come to the conclusion that there's hope in you yet, where there isn't for gay people. Bisexuals haven't tossed out the baby with the bath. Straight people don't even think about sexuality, sexual orientation, or any of those things most of the time.

I've never really thought that much about what determines our sexuality, but sometimes I think it might be genetic. I have one sister who's a lesbian, too, for what that's worth. Maybe there is something in our parents' genes that influenced our behavior. I'll have to ask her what she thinks about that. Because of the four-year difference in our ages, we were brought up in different ways. We had the same mother and father, but I was the one who had to fight for things. By the time my sister wanted to wear lipstick or stay up late at night, they couldn't have cared less. The two of us have become a lot tighter since we got out of school, but she is not a lesbian because she's following in my footsteps. We weren't even living in the same section of the country when we individually began to relate to other women.

"What would be great is if sexual expression didn't matter. One of the other things that has retarded this is the church. The pressure we get from that institution is really pervasive. I was a churchgoer every Sunday until I began relating to women. And then I stopped. At first I felt a void in my life, but since then I've taken a broader look at religion and put it in its proper perspective. There is no way for a person who relates to members of the same sex to enter a church without feeling guilty. We're not doing what is preached every single Sunday of the year.

"I'd like to see things change, but I don't know how possible it is. I'm back more with my women friends now, and that's the way I'll continue. I learned more about myself by seeing that man, and maybe that's why bisexual women keep a few in their lives. Now I won't hop in as readily and put down bisexual women. I don't think I ever did, but if some years from now I find myself doing it, I'll stop. If nothing else, I tried it but didn't like it. Maybe it was the particular man, but he brought back so many memories of incomplete relationships I'd had when I was much younger. Now I had the advantage of knowing how good it can be to love a woman. I know all the emotional help another woman can offer me. The comparison between the two was just too stark to make me want to rush back into male/female situations. Bisexual women have my support and understanding. Perhaps they've discovered something that I didn't. I wish them luck."

8.

Bisexual Soundings

When bisexual women are not completely ignored by most of society, their life-styles are misinterpreted. In the respondents' estimation this has happened because those in the majority in anything—whether it is ethnic background, political affiliation, dietary habits, or sexual orientation—do not allocate the energy required to understand those different from themselves. While overtly making the effort in some areas, sexuality continues to be approached guardedly. Puritanical attitudes persist toward anyone straying from the heterosexual course, and laws codify those attitudes.

Not only must they be heterosexual, but they are discouraged and even forbidden to experiment within those confines. Throughout almost the entire United States it is still illegal for consenting adults to practice cunnilingus and fellatio. Instead of amending the law, it is enforced at whim, especially to harrass homosexuals. Many women are also denied control over their own bodies. A number of states have not legalized abortion, and Right-to-Lifers are turning the Supreme Court decision into a political issue. With no completely safe method of birth control for women involved in heterosexual relationships, if a woman does conceive and wants to have child she must follow societal dictates on this point as well. Trying to locate a doctor who will deliver a baby in the woman's home calls for a diligent search, and midwifery is against the law in most areas.

The restrictions placed on all people by the majority are alarming. Many bisexual women believe that although they are seen as a threat by some females, men feel threatened to an even greater degree. This is a male-run nation. Men make and enforce the laws. Men grant or repress women's sexuality from what they view as right and good for them, not for women. Many resist the possibility of equality because it means they will have to give up much of the power they hold. By keeping women in their traditional place, men remain secure in positions of authority.

The media are reflectors of our culture. Much of our information, knowledge, and beliefs are molded by this male-dominated bastion. The reporters bring with them not an objective eye but all the biases of our country. Women's issues are not as newsworthy as men's. When female-related topics are covered, it is often with levity. Women's sexuality is far down the list of priorities.

Many women interviewed for this book stated that if the media men were forced to deal with women as sexual entities, they would be hardpressed. Male fears of emasculation would surface, their potency lessen. Jackie believes the media have only recently acknowledged the existence of homosexuality, with men getting the majority of the press. Bisexuality is not recognized as another alternative, and therefore there have been minimal collective responses to this option. "Soon there'll be more glimmers of our existence," Jackie stated, "and I think we'll have wider interest and acceptance than the gay community. We don't completely reject the heterosexual concept. Our activities can be explained away fairly readily as temporary waverings from a straight life. This isn't the case, but it's something more people can identify with. Then, as everybody becomes tuned into their own sexuality, there'll be greater understanding and maybe even a little compassion. We all want pleasure and this, bisexuality, is one more outlet to think about."

Most respondents are not as optimistic as Jackie. They perceive the media treatment as superficial and contradictory as they hear themselves referred to as experimenters at best, mentally unbalanced sensation-seekers at worst. One impression, they think, that is relayed is that bisexual women are promiscuous, exciting, hot items. The sum total of their identities is overshadowed by the sexual—as if their only thoughts or emotions were sex-related. Unanimously, the bisexual women wish they could call a halt to this type of exploitation. They are individuals, people, multifaceted beings, not one-dimensional automatons.

Another societal attitude frequently voiced is that bisexual women are to be pitied because of their psychological problems. Their turning to both men and women for love, gratification, and attention is interpreted as mental imbalance, and some psychologists maintain that the results are incomplete relationships with everybody.

To bisexual women neither of these views is valid. The women discussed why their murky image has been further distorted by society and what they feel people should understand about a bisexual life-style.

Fran was representative. "Stories always portray us in a horrible way. We're held up as sex-starved maniacs. Other articles in news magazines that try to have a more objective coverage stress how unhappy we are. Their conclusion is that this isn't a good, wholesome way of life. Being bisexual is a copout, manipulative, or evil. I don't think we're taken at all seriously. Every time I read something like that I get so irritated. I want to write a letter to the editor and say, 'Where did you dig up the people to interview? Ask me, for a change.'

"I can just imagine the whole scenario in the newsroom. 'Hey, fellas, let's do a piece on people who swing both ways. Something different for a change. We're tired of all this gay rights stuff. Bisexuality is something more offbeat, bizarre. Make a few quick calls and we'll see if we can fit it in. Wow, interviews with a couple, real live bisexuals!' It's pure hoopla.

"What I'd most like people who aren't bisexual to know is that this isn't a fad. They can't close their eyes and hope we'll go away, because we won't. Throughout history there's always been bisexuality. The only difference is in how accepted it is. I'm not going to hurt anyone. I don't criticize people unlike myself and force my life-style down their throats. I'm not sick. I'm not telling lies. Both men and women are important to me, and I won't forget about one for the other. I'm not in transition.

"All I want is the right to live my life as I see fit. Get rid of the laws. Get rid of the judgmental attitudes. I'm no better or worse than anyone else. I'm just a little different. To my way of thinking, that should make me more interesting."

We are an opinionated nation, one that defines and categorizes everything with value judgments tacked on. Patricia wishes people would have a less slanted interest in bisexuality. "Live and let live is what should be happening, but it isn't. I think everyone should try to learn from others before immediately putting them down for doing what brings them pleasure. Observers and commentators shouldn't let us get to them so much. The television people pick up on just one small part of our lives, that we sexually relate to men and women. They blow that up to the point that people must think we spend all of our time on our backs—or fronts, depending on what time the TV show is aired—and how scandalous they think they can be.

"We are human beings. We're not all neurotic, or at least any more so than the rest of the folks around. People are always throwing out biblical quotations to prove how God intended men and women to be sexually intimate, not members of the same sex. Well, why do they suddenly close their Bibles when it comes to such words as 'judge not lest ye shall be judged.' Or why not bring out that old favorite, 'Let he who is without sin cast the first stone.' No, they don't want to think about those parts that they can't use as ammunition against us. A friend of mine always says, 'What goes around comes around.' By that she means what you do and feel towards others will be duplicated. If you mistreat someone, sooner or later it will come back to you, and you'll be the one suffering. Maybe those who're most judgmental are most threatened because they're afraid of their own sexuality."

Liv did not speak with Patricia's irritation. She was philosophical in presenting her theories on the societal overview of bisexuality. Many respondents agreed with her comments that the public's primary attitude to bisexuality can be summed up as nonexistent. Liv said, "We're invisible to most people, so they have no opinions one way or the other. They can't be hurt by what they don't know, so they turn their backs on us. If people said, 'Yes, there are some who are bisexual,' then they'd have to deal with us. We'd be one more disturbing factor, and this world is already cluttered with confusing elements. Life is a lot simpler when you ignore things that make you feel uneasy. I could never understand people who lavished attention on their dogs and were rotten to their kids. Finally I decided it was best just not to think about it. People do the same with us. If they're not bisexual, it's a life-style that may be hard to comprehend. Why bother, when their lives are already complicated.

"Being bisexual is part of me. It's integrated into my total character. I first started thinking about it ten years ago when one of my high school teachers brought it up. She said if I really want to relate to people, bisexuality was how to do it. She and I aren't saying that everyone should be bisexual, but I think people should start realizing how much society has pressured them to behave sexually in a certain way. They should start coming to grips with the fact that all facets of their character are conditioned by what they get through the family, church, school, and, ultimately, the media. Nothing can ever change or progress until they try shedding themselves of some of that conditioning. Then they can more honestly approach what their true sexual feelings are. At least I'd wish they'd be cognizant that most people in America have been terribly trapped and programmed. And it's a limiting factor.

"When you become aware of that, you become able to reach out beyond it. Then you can discover how you chose to relate; what's best for you. Otherwise you can get caught in the bind of feeling you have to interact sexually in one certain way—if you don't find fulfillment in it, then everything falls down. You feel inadequate because you're not fulfilled. You do eccentric things to try and find fulfillment and hate yourself for them. Rather you should say, 'It doesn't have to be this way. I have numerous options of how I can relate to different people.' Or you may even learn you have to grow from within first, remain celibate for awhile until you know more about yourself. You can be a mixture of sexual expressions. If we looked at relationships from differing standpoints, then I think we'd have a better place to live."

Grace mixed dismay and hope when she talked about society's approach to bisexual women. In her words, "Bisexuality is a viable life-style which is on the uprise, especially among women. Women are getting more in touch with themselves. While exploring the minds of our sisters, we discovered it's as important to discover their bodies."

Although more of those interviewed believe you should follow what is best for you in terms of your sexual orientation, Grace represented the minority theory that bisexuality is the normal condition and all else is a perversion, a mutation. "You're either both or none," she said. "I can't see quibbling over whether it's a male or female body if the spirit is there. I know what I've just said will outrage some, but it's what I believe. Quite possibly the day will come when more feel this way.

"No one way of living is entirely right any more than another way is all wrong. I'll give that much.

I don't change sex partners with the regularity I change clothes. Sex between people has more meaning than a handshake. Sometimes people put too much emphasis on sex. Making love to a person is a positive way of reinforcing and extending your affection for them. Why does it freak out all those heterosexuals when that's exactly what they're doing except they're restricting themselves to the opposite sex? They've lopped off half the population. Now I mean is that right or normal? 'Stay away from me, you've got breasts. You don't have a beard, so I can't kiss you. I can't hold you and tell you what a special person you are, how glad I am that you're in my life. Society says it's okay to kiss your cheek, you wonderful woman, but I can't kiss your genitals. Society says I must find a man for that.' I want to know women as thoroughly and intimately as I know men. Why should I be punished for that? Why should people make me feel I'm doing something dirty or sick? Why is this something I've got to hide from my family? What are we as a nation doing to ourselves?

"I've spent the majority of my life listening to straight society and their highly touted values. Look what's happening. Their divorce rate is sky-rocketing. Their kids are suffering from their trampoline existences. Let's see, if it's the third weekend it must be daddy's day to see the offspring. They're having nervous breakdowns. Why must they push their trips on me to the extent I sometimes question my own sanity? They're searching just as earnestly for peace and happiness and having the same troubles finding it. Now give me and other bisexual women a little equal time. Not even equal, just admit that not everything in straight people's lives is working. Maybe they don't hold the key to the mysteries of life and human relationships after all. I'm not saying we do, but we might have some additional clues because we've freed ourselves from this holy tenet to be exclusively straight that they honor as the be-all and end-all. I get mad, then amused, and finally move on to boredom. I'm happy. Are they?"

Maria saw change coming in our culture, but an initial step is shoving aside the label syndrome. By dividing people into categories we remove the human element, and that is indicative of the problem. Instead of examining individuals, we select the most appropriate title and then wrap all our preconceived notions associated with that word around the person. "Society gets caught up in identification and categorizing," Maria said. "They've got to put everything in one of two classifications. What two? Well, there's male and female. There's heterosexual and homosexual, or the liberals who think they're really surging ahead of everyone else will say 'straight' or 'gay.' They did the same thing when Negroes were transformed into blacks and Indians became Native Americans. We've got to have a title, a pigeonhole so people will know how to respond to us. And all this boils down to is the name game is a big part of the trouble.

"Why do we feel we have to divide everyone up like so many slices of a pie? When you do that, you open yourself up to other disastrous stuff like the 'we's' and the 'they's.' Let's forget about all that garbage. What I'd hope would come through all these comments is that everyone would be better off if they said, 'People are people are people.' Let's learn and love as the spirit moves us."

If the bisexual women could project into the future, they would envision an androgynous culture. Cindy spoke for many: "Androgyny is the qualities of masculine and feminine in one personality. Both men and women can be aggressive and passive, independent and dependent in differing degrees depending on their experiences and makeup. I feel what we should begin doing is getting out of the stereotype of saying man's role versus woman's. We should work on eliminating that distinction. Everyone should be open to do whatever they want to, according to their own personal needs. If we were to develop a more androgynous society, everyone would benefit. We should value all types of sexual expression as long as they aren't harmful to others.

"Obviously I'm not condoning rape or child molesting or any of those other abominations, but I don't think of them as sexual expression. They're vicious, demented outlets. Love between people should receive our energy, and making love should became a natural thing, to be praised instead of condemned."

What the respondents also emphasize is that no one, regardless of sexual orientation, should be made to feel uncomfortable or penalized in any way. A bisexual life-style is only one alternative, not applicable to everyone. Do what makes you the most balanced and contented, rather than acquiesce to external pressures. Although the bisexual women do not know all the answers of relating to individuals, gender aside, they are consciously making the effort to change. The women interviewed are working through the problems of role-playing when with men, trying to be aware of and eliminate the tendency to see women as competition. They want to be people-oriented people. They feel they have extra insight into themselves and others because of their unique lives. With each person they meet, there is the possibility of complete interaction. They dream of a better, more humane world.

Societal attitudes and sexual mores have been changing and evolving. The women predicted that in the future this process will gather speed. An initial step will be made when the public recognizes that the bisexual population is larger than suspected. While Dr. Wardell Pomeroy puts the figure at 10 percent of all men and 5 percent of women, those interviewed for this book feel it is more prevalent among women. Some believe as many as 20 percent of all women could be defined as bisexual, and they base this percentage on several factors. Often women who relate to both sexes are unfamiliar with the concept of bisexuality. Thus they have not affixed that precise word to their lifestyle. Others want to avoid the ramifications of admitting to themselves and friends that they love women as well as men. Their purpose is better served by remaining silent about their sexual orientation.

Many people do not realize or will not admit the impact of feminism. In general the women felt that those in the movement are not degrading men or proselytizing intimacies with their sisters but, by providing the atmosphere to question roles and relationships, they are enabling more women to explore and understand their sexuality. No one interviewed had any sense of being forced or pressured into another life-style. They simply became aware of the possibility. People do not magically "convert" to bisexuality.

The increasing number of discussion groups for bisexual women are sponsored mainly by feminist organizations, and the women felt these groups will continue to multiply as more avow both the necessity for them and the alternative that bisexuality represents. They saw a need for supportive environments in which women can strengthen their sense of self while educating others.

Another point many of the women made is that a certain portion of women are and would be bisexual, feminism or not. This has been true through the centuries and would hold for the present and future.

Even though bisexual women did not foresee becoming as organized or united as their gay counterparts, they thought they would soon have a more visible, vocal place—first within the women's movement and then in society in general. Simultaneously, they hoped to learn from the struggles of other minorities. They realized that as their visibility increased their actions and activities would create both fear and disdain. While they did not foresee bisexual rights candidates, platforms, rallies, lobbyists, and the like, they did feel more will recognize them and their concerns.

As the word itself appears more frequently in print, the public becomes familiar with this previously hidden aspect of sexuality. Cases such as that of Ensign Vernon Berg, a naval academy graduate who fought dismissal from the service, will not be a rarity. During the past seven years, Berg stated, he has engaged in both homosexual and heterosexual activities. All of the men he sexually related to were civilians, yet the military wanted him out because its personnel "should be able to live in close association" minus contact with "a homosexual atmosphere." Berg argued he should be evaluated on his ability to perform his job as a naval officer while keeping his sex life separate. Although this case focuses on the individual's intimacies with members of the same sex, it does publicize the existence of this life-style. A few years ago the term bisexual would not have even appeared.

Many of the women agreed that bisexuals are subject to less violent reactions than are some members of the gay community, because they have a lower profile. By not entirely rejecting the relating patterns of the majority, alliance can be assumed at least on one level. As Barbara said, "The vanguard won't ever be as outlandish as the drag queens or the heavy-duty separatists. While some gay people mimic the worst characteristics of the opposite sex, we tend to hunt for the best parts of male and female to embrace. Since we want to mix both together, we don't have the extremes. I'm not saying all bisexual women are alike; that's ridiculous. But we're closer to the middle of the continuum sexually and in the way we dress and act in public so we won't ever stand out to the same extent. We don't flaunt our sexuality in the same manner, because we're not making that kind of statement. Maybe it's not as honest as the radical gay people, but we'll never wear our sexual orientation on our sleeves the way some of them do. Basically I'd guess that most of us look pretty straight, so Aunt Matilda and Uncle Fred out there in the Midwest don't really know what we're up to. We don't scare or bewilder them in the same way the queens and dykes do."

To further this process of restructuring moral standards and attitudes, everyone must at least concede that women are sexual beings. Emotional, physical, and legal control over their bodies must be granted. Some states, such as California, are taking timid steps toward this goal, but all agree that more widespread action is needed. The women felt all forms of sexual expression between consenting people should be allowed, rather than technically forbidden and merely tolerated.

Many respondents felt that much of the anguish people experience when examining their sexuality is church-inspired. While a few priests, ministers, and rabbis on the local level have withdrawn their blanket condemnation of masturbation, premarital sex, and homosexual activities, the hierarchy remains steadfast in its opposition. They cite the 1976 "Declaration on Certain Questions Concerning Sexual Ethics" which was reviewed and approved by Pope Paul as one example of this continuing pressure. Theologians must realize the masses they are losing with these harsh doctrines. These attitudes, the women believed, place unnatural restrictions on all people. They induce guilt and anxiety. A thorough reevaluation of these dogmas must occur.

They were convinced that bisexuality would not contribute to the downfall of marriage. Although at present the institution seems close to being placed in the endangered species category, it has not and will not be affected by any increase in bisexuality. Those who feel all alternate forms of sexuality are a threat to marriage are looking for a convenient scapegoat. In cultures where bisexuality is accepted, heterosexuality is still more prevalent. The options are simply increased, the fear removed. Sociologists, theologians, anthropologists, and other commentators have various opinions on why the divorce rate broke the one million mark in 1975, but none blamed it on bisexuality.

Bisexual women are not alone in feeling that everyone should not be pressured to marry and produce children. No adult should be oppressed for remaining single. As Doris said, "In my utopia no one would be put down for doing what was best for him or her. Everyone shouldn't go to college. Everyone can't have a white-collar job. We're learning that. Some of us have to do different things in order for society to work. Nothing should be held up as better so that those not doing it feel badly about themselves. There's just as much dignity in cleaning up streets as cleaning up business problems.

"Now carry that a few steps on. Marriage isn't right for everybody. Being straight just doesn't fit the whole world. We should be delighted by diversity. Sexual orientation is so overrated. Society isn't going to come crashing down around our heads because everyone doesn't accept the exclusive heterosexual role.

"When I was a kid I was brought up on the melting-pot theory. All those people from different countries came here and were synthesized, processed, and pounded out until they conformed to the 'American Way.' But then we looked around our major cities. Italians, Germans, blacks, Puerto Ricans, Chicanos— all living in separate sections; all with their own lists of beliefs. It weirded out a lot of people, but we're catching on now. We're flowing a little better. People have the right to maintain their own identities. Let's do that in personality and sexuality, too.

"I heard a radio call-in program where a leader from the gay movement was being interviewed. Someone asked if the governor of California, Jerry Brown, was gay. Boy! Just because he's never married, that was the conclusion the listener had. What the caller was doing was typical of many individuals. If you don't get married by the time you're twenty-five or thirty, obviously there's something wrong with you, or you're probably gay. It just doesn't make sense to me. Freedom, human and emotional freedom, is my utopia. That's what it's all about."

Stripping away the layers of mystique helps everyone develop a healthier attitude toward sexual expression. But, the women agreed, there are limits. They did not recommend sexual relations in situations that would infringe upon the rights of others. What they desired was acceptance to privately relate to whomever they want.

The majority of those interviewed for this book felt we should move toward a more rounded, androgynous society free of all sex-role stereotyping. Cindy touched upon this in her concluding remarks. A summary of the other responses reveals the general feeling that in order for society to advance, it will be necessary to work at blending and making intelligent application of the best attributes of each sex. While it may be difficult for many men and even some women to accept, it is a fact that skill in housework is not a sex-linked characteristic. The capability of excelling in physics is not preordained only in men. As traditional roles are challenged, the rigid aspects of gender-defining can be dissolved.

The women point out that females are not genetically more emotionally brittle than males. Also, they can be just as forceful, practical, and strong as any man. A good cry is a release for everyone, regardless of gender. Nurturing is inherent in all people, not a task assigned to one sex above the other. As we edge closer toward an androgynous society, the women believe the value of interpersonal relationships will increase. The worth of honest and open friendships will rate higher than material success. Their ultimate goal is acceptance of whatever sexual orientation an individual chooses.

Conclusions about bisexual women and their lifestyles are for the reader to make. I did not edit out the commentaries that showed bisexual women in a negative light any more than I selected only those reiterating the positive side. As one respondent stated, I recorded their words "warts and all." Attitudes about human sexuality are changing. There are numerous options, and no single path is the right way for everyone. The women interviewed for this book ask only that they, and all people, be accorded the freedom of emotional and sexual interaction.

Bibliography

Barbach, Lonnie Garfield. *For Yourself: The Fulfillment of Female Sexuality, A Guide to Orgasmic Response.* Garden City: Doubleday, 1975.

Bengis, Ingrid. *Combat in the Erogenous Zone.* New York: Knopf, 1972.

Boston Women's Health Collective. *Our Bodies, Ourselves: A Book by and for Women.* New York: Simon & Schuster, 1971.

Brecher, Ruth and Brecher, Edward. *An Analysis of Human Sexual Response.* New York, New American Library, 1966.

Colton, Helen. *Sex after the Sexual Revolution.* New York: Association, 1972.

Davis, Elizabeth Gould. *The First Sex.* New York: Putnam's, 1971.

Diner, Helen. *Mothers and Amazons: The First Feminine History of Culture.* New York: Julian Press, 1965.

Dodson, Betty. *Liberating Masturbation.* New York: Bodysex Designs, 1974.

Falk, Ruth. *Woman Loving: A Journey Toward Becoming an Independent Woman.* New York: Random House/Berkeley, The Bookworks, 1975.

Ford, Clellan S., and Beach, Frank A. *Patterns of Sexual Behavior.* New York: Harper & Row, 1951.

Friday, Nancy. *My Secret Garden: Women's Sexual Fantasies.* New York: Trident, 1973.

Gagnon, John H., and Simon, William. *Sexual Conduct: The Social Sources of Human Sexuality*. Chicago: Aldine, 1973.

Gearhart, Sally, and Johnson, William, eds. *Loving Women/ Loving Men: Gay Liberation and the Church*. San Francisco: Glide, 1974.

Hammer, Signe, ed. *Women: Body and Culture*. New York: Harper & Row, 1975.

Heilbrun, Carolyn G. *Toward a Recognition of Androgyny*. New York: Knopf, 1973.

Johnston, Jill. *Lesbian Nation: The Feminist Solution*. New York: Simon & Schuster, 1973.

Kinsey, Alfred C., et al. *Sexual Behavior in the Human Female*. Philadelphia: W. B. Saunders, 1953.

Klaich, Dolores. *Woman + Woman: Attitudes Toward Lesbianism*. New York: Simon & Schuster, 1974.

Love, Barbara, and Abbot, Sidney. *Sappho was a Right-on Woman: A Liberated View of Lesbianism*. New York: Stein & Day, 1972.

Ludovici, Lawrence James. *The Final Inequality: A Critical Assessment of Women's Sexual Role in Society*. New York: W. W. Norton, 1965.

Martin, Del, and Lyon, Phyllis. *Lesbian/Woman*. San Francisco: Glide, 1972.

Masters, William H., and Johnson, Virginia E. *Human Sexual Inadequacy*. Boston: Little, Brown, 1970.

————. *The Pleasure Bond: A New Look at Sexuality and Commitment*. Boston: Little, Brown, 1974.

Mead, Margaret. *Male and Female: A Study of the Sexes in a Changing World*. New York: W. Morrow, 1949.

Mercer, J. D. *They Walk in Shadow: A Study of Sexual Variations with Emphasis on the Ambisexual and Homosexual Components and Our Contemporary Sex Laws*. New York: Comet, 1959.

Miller, Jean Baker, ed. *Psychoanalysis and Women*. Baltimore: Penguin, 1973.

Millett, Kate. *Flying*. New York: Knopf, 1974.

Money, John, and Ehrhardt, Anke A. *Man and Woman Boy and Girl: Differentiation and Dimorphism of Gender Identity from Conception to Maturity*. Baltimore: Johns Hopkins University, 1972.

Nicolson, Nigel. *Portrait of a Marriage*. New York: Atheneum, 1973.

Nomadic Sisters and Hammond, Victoria. *Loving Women*. San Francisco: Up Press, 1975.

Ramer, Leonard V. *Your Sexual Bill of Rights: An Analysis of the Harmful Effects of Sexual Prohibitions*. New York: Exposition, 1973.

Reich, Wilhelm. *The Function of the Orgasm*. New York: Noonday, 1961.

Roszak, Betty, and Roszak, Theodore, eds. *Masculine/Feminine: Readings in Sexual Mythology and the Liberation of Women*. New York: Harper & Row, 1969.

Rush, Anne Kent. *Getting Clear: Body Work for Women*. New York: Random House/Berkeley, The Bookworks, 1973.

Schaefer, Leah Cahan. *Women and Sex: Sexual Experiences and Reactions of a Group of Thirty Women as Told to a Female Psychotherapist*. New York: Pantheon, 1973.

Seaman, Barbara. *Free and Female: The New Sexual Role of Women*. New York: Coward-McCann & Geoghegan, 1972.

Sherfey, Mary J. *The Nature and Evolution of Female Sexuality*. New York: Random House, 1972.

Smith, James R., and Smith, Lynn G. *Beyond Monogamy*. Baltimore: Johns Hopkins University, 1974.

Teal, Donn. *The Gay Militants*. New York: Stein & Day, 1971.

Wolff, Charlotte. *Love between Women*. New York: St. Martin's, 1971.

Wysor, Bettie. *The Lesbian Myth*. New York: Random House, 1974.

Index

SCIENCE FICTION MASTERPIECES